Key issues in economics and business

Government and the economy

Key Issues in Economics and Business

Series editors: Alan Griffiths, Keith Pye and Stuart Wall

Government
and the economy

K. Bain
P.G.A. Howells

94

Longman
London and New York

Longman Group UK Limited
Longman House, Burnt Mill, Harlow
Essex CM20 2JE, England
and Associated companies throughout the world

*Published in the United States of America
by Longman Inc., New York*

© Longman Group UK Limited 1987

First published 1987

British Library Cataloguing in Publication Data
Bain, K.
   Government and the economy. – (Key issues
   in economics and business)
   1. Economic policy
   I. Title   II. Howells, P.G.A.
   III. Series
   330.9182′1   HD87
   ISBN 0-582-29670-6

Library of Congress Cataloging in Publication Data
Bain, K., 1942–
   Government and the economy.

   (Key issues in economics and business)
   Bibliography: p.
   Includes index.
   1. Economic policy. I. Howells, P.G.A.,
1947–   . II. Title. III. Series.
HD82.B217   1986   338.9   86-3025
ISBN 0-582-29670-6

Set in Linotron 202 10/11 pt Plantin
Produced by Longman Group (FE) Limited
Printed in Hong Kong

Contents

Editors' preface

Each title in this series takes a particular area of economics or business studies and subjects it to rather more scrutiny than is possible in most introductory textbooks. Part one of each book concentrates on the key issues which present themselves for investigation or enquiry. It is hoped that a careful analysis of principle and date will save the reader considerable 'search time'. The issues selected will be those which are frequently the subject of examination questions at 'A' level, on professional courses and at the start of an undergraduate programme. At the end of each chapter, or group of chapters, a range of past questions will be presented to indicate the type of question the student is often expected to answer. Part two of each book presents specimen answers/worked examples to the questions outlined in part one. Except where worked examples are essential, the main objective will be to help students identify that part of their acquired knowledge which could be used in answering particular questions. A guide to sources of current information and data will help those who wish themselves to keep abreast of current developments or who intend to undertake essays/projects or dissertations in that particular area of economics or business.

Alan Griffiths
Keith Pye
Stuart Wall

Acknowledgements

The ideas expressed in this text are the product of many influences. Among the most valuable have been the discussions with colleagues, with our students and with visitors to the North East London Polytechnic conferences for students and teachers of 'A'-level economics. We acknowledge this with pleasure and with thanks.

In the latter stages of preparation we received particularly helpful comment and advice from Michael Marshall, Peter Mottershead and Frank Skuse. For their generosity we are especially grateful. We want also to thank the editors of this series, especially Stuart Wall for his meticulous attention to detail and for his constant encouragement. The only parts of this text of which we feel confidently the originators, are the errors.

We are grateful to the following for permission to use copyright material:

Bank of England for table 6.2; Grafton Books (A Division of the Collins Publishing Group) for table 3.2; the Controller, Her Majesty's Stationery Office for tables 2.1, 2.2, 3.1, 5.1, 6.1;

and the following Examination Boards for permission to reproduce questions from past examination papers:

The Associated Examining Board; The Institute of Bankers; The Institute of Chartered Secretaries and Administrators; The Institute of Cost and Management Accountants; Joint Matriculation Board; Oxford and Cambridge Schools Examination Board; University of London School Examinations Board; University of Oxford Delegacy of Local Examinations; Welsh Joint Education Committee.

Any answers or hints on answers are the sole responsibility of the authors and have not been provided or approved by the above Examination Boards.

List of Abbreviations

Throughout the text the following abbreviations have been used to identify the examination bodies who have been kind enough to let us use their past examination questions:

ACA	Association of Certified Accountants
AEB	Associated Examining Board
ICMA	Institute of Cost and Management Accountants
ICSA	Institute of Chartered Secretaries and Administrators
I of B	Institute of Bankers
JMB	The Joint Metriculation Board
London	University Entrance and Schools Examination Council of the University of London
Oxford & Cambridge	Oxford & Cambridge Schools Examination Board
Oxford	Oxford Delegacy of Local Examinations
WJEC	Welsh Joint Examination Committee

Part one

Chapter one
The mixed economy

One of the major developments over the course of this century has been the growth in the size and importance of government in all western market economies. This growth has become a major area of controversy in economics and politics, especially over the past decade, with an increase in support for the notion that the role of government in the economy should be drastically reduced (though the practice has not always matched up to the theory).

We can begin our examination of the issue by looking at just how large government has become. We can then go on to consider the general arguments concerning the desirable extent of government participation within market economies.

1.1 Measuring the size of government

There can be no single measure of the size of government – much depends on the reason for one's interest in it. Considerable differences among measurements may also arise because of variations in the accounting definitions used. It is possible, however, to obtain an idea of the extent of the growth in government over the years by looking separately at measures of expenditure, taxation and employment.

1.1.1 Government expenditure

Growth in the size of government expenditure can be put forward as one indicator of increased government involvement in market economies. It is inadequate in many ways since some important actions by government may involve very little expenditure (for example, employment protection legislation and the enforcement of health and safety regulations) whereas other items of expenditure imply very little control by government of market forces (advertising to persuade people to drive more safely or to buy shares in an industry about to be de-nationalised). Still, greater expenditure does suggest greater involvement.

Obviously, however, government expenditure has grown very rapidly because of the inflation which has occurred. We could attempt to use price indices to remove the impact of inflation on the figures and try to see how much government expenditure has grown in real terms. But this would remain misleading because of the very large increase which has occurred in real income in the economy. A constant level of real government expenditure over a period in which real incomes rose as a result of economic growth might suggest that government influence in the economy was actually falling. It has, therefore, been accepted that the best expenditure measure is to take government expenditure *as a percentage of* some indicator of total national income or national product.

Now, however, even more problems present themselves. We have difficulties in knowing what to include in government expenditure and what to leave out. Further, we can use any one of several measures of national income. Finally, we can argue about whether or not inflation has had a different impact on public expenditure than on private expenditure. Let us take these problems one at a time.

Components of government expenditure

The first problem is what to include under the heading of government expenditure. Perhaps the major difference of opinion here concerns **transfer payments**. It is possible to argue that we should only be interested in those elements of government expenditure which imply control of resources. We could say that if a government taxes citizen A and transfers the proceeds of the tax to citizen B, say in the form of a pension, then the decision as to which goods and services will be purchased and hence produced still rests with a private individual. All that government has done is to act as an agent in bringing about the distribution of income which society wants. This is quite different from using the proceeds of the tax on citizen A directly to build missiles or hospitals, in which case the government really would be deciding how the nation's scarce resources should be used. It is therefore argued that lumping transfer payments together with other types of expenditure only confuses separate issues, and that it is better to omit transfer payments from measures of government expenditure.

A counter-argument might be: (a) that in the case of transfer payments the government has still influenced the way resources will be used since citizen B may have different demands from citizen A; (b) that it is the market which should determine income distribution as well as patterns of production, with an implication here being that government intervention in altering income distribution would be likely to lead to inefficiencies in the use of resources by influencing A's and B's incentives to work.

It should be noted that if this counter-argument is accepted and transfer payments are included in government expenditure, we finish up with a rather odd ratio. Since none of the usual measures of national income (the denominator of the ratio) includes transfer payments, the ratio could become larger than 100 per cent.

The size of transfer payments and thus the importance of the argument as to whether or not they should be included, is shown in Table 1.1.

The treatment of the **nationalised industries** is also a worry. We could propose that nationalised industries act like those of the

Table 1.1 Composition of UK general government expenditure 1950–85

Expenditure on goods and services			*Current and capital transfers*	
Year	*£ m.*	*% of total*	*£ m.*	*% of total*
1950	2,587	57.2	1,935	42.8
1955	3,928	60.7	2,538	39.3
1960	5,067	56.7	3,865	43.3
1965	7,487	56.3	5,823	43.7
1970	11,451	54.8	9,431	45.2
1975	28,078	54.5	23,475	45.5
1980	54,458	52.3	49,652	47.7
1981	59,872	51.2	57,094	48.8
1982	64,890	50.4	63,754	49.6
1983*	71,612	51.7	66,879	48.3
1984*	75,904	52.2	69,457	47.8
1985	81,271	51.5	76,608	48.5

* Figures from 1983 on for transfers are distorted by the subtraction of the proceeds of the sale of public assets.
Source: Economic Trends Annual supplements

private sector in all ways related to the use of resources, with consumers playing a major role in deciding what is produced. We could then claim that they should be included in government expenditure only to the extent to which they receive subsidies from central government. The opposite position would be that since nationalised industries are part of the public sector, *all* of their expenditures should be counted as part of government expenditure. This would give a very large figure for government expenditure indeed. Intermediate positions are possible: for example, we might include all the nationalised industries' *investment* expenditure and exclude the rest.

The way in which the government **implements** its policy decisions may also affect the figures. Imagine, for example, that a government decides to subsidise industries in a poor region of the country. If it chooses to do this by providing cash subsidies, then the figure for government expenditure goes up; if it chooses instead to give tax allowances (sometimes called tax expenditures) to companies, then government expenditure does not rise.

Finally, **accounting conventions** are important in determining which items to include in government expenditure. An example of this can be seen in the treatment of the proceeds of the sale of public assets. The government accounts have been showing these as reductions in expenditure. One could equally justify treating them as additions to revenue. The result of doing so would be to produce a higher figure for government expenditure.

Definitions of national income
The second problem we have with our ration relates to the denominator. There are many available measures of a country's income – GDP (gross domestic product) at factor cost; GDP at market prices; GNP (gross national product) at factor cost; national income, that is NNP (net national product) at factor cost, and so on. Arguments can be made for each of them. For instance, if we were principally interested in domestic employment and hence domestic output, then we would choose GDP. If we thought that changes in government taxation policy, such as a switch from direct to indirect taxation, had an impact upon market prices, we might prefer to use as our measure GDP *at factor cost*. The difference which is made to the ratio by changing the denominator is very large as is shown in Table 1.2.

Treatment of inflation
Our final problem, which applies only to the resource-using

5

Government and the economy

Table 1.2 UK public expenditure ratios
1984

General government expenditure as percentage of:	%
GDP at factor cost	52.4
GDP at market prices	45.1
GNP at factor cost	51.8
National income	60.0

Sources: *Economic Trends* Annual Supplement 1985;
UK National Accounts 1985

component of government expenditure, is perhaps the trickiest. This hinges on the notion that on average the commodities produced by the public sector are different in nature from those produced by the private sector. The suggestion is that more of the satisfaction which consumers obtain from publicly provided goods and services comes *directly* from the way in which goods and services are produced than is the case with private sector goods and services. Thus labour can be less readily replaced by machines in the public sector than in the private sector. A simple way of thinking of this distinction among different types of commodities is to compare the relative ease of replacing production line workers by robots with replacing hospital doctors by robots. As a result, this argument continues, labour productivity will rise more slowly in the public sector than in the private sector. If workers receive the same increases in wage rates in the two sectors, then public sector commodities will, over time, become *relatively more expensive*.

It follows that if the public sector is to continue to provide the same proportion of total product of the economy, it will need to spend a steadily higher proportion of total expenditure. One of the advantages of using a *ratio* as our measure of government expenditure is that it overcomes the problem of inflation, since the numerator and the denominator are valued using the same year's prices. Now, however, we are saying that this is inadequate, since different rates of inflation apply to the two sectors. A truer picture would then be obtained if we were to deflate government expenditure in the numerator of our ratio, by a *different* (and higher) price index than national income in the denominator, since the latter

Table 1.3 UK general government expenditure in relation to GDP at factor cost 1955–85

Year	General government expenditure (£ m.)	GDP at factor cost (£ m.)	Government expenditure as % of GDP
1955	6.5	16.9	38.5
1965	13.3	31.5	42.2
1975	51.6	95.8	53.9
1980	104.1	199.1	52.3
1981	117.0	217.6	53.8
1982	128.5	235.5	54.6
1983*	138.5	257.2	53.9
1984*	145.4	277.3	52.4
1985*	157.8	302.8	52.1

* Government expenditure figures for these years are reduced by
the proceeds of the sale of public assets.
Source: Economic Trends

includes both public and private sectors. This would tend to reduce the measured growth of the public sector.

In summary, we can say that although almost all methods of measurement indicate a very large growth over the past century in government expenditure as a proportion of total output, the precise figures are very difficult to interpret. Table 1.3 provides one set of figures with the upward trend in the ratio clearly visible.

Certainly, any attempt to compare the size of government in different countries on the basis of government expenditure raises very many problems since the structure of government and the nature of expenditure differ, as do definitions and accounting practices used in the presentation of official statistics.

1.1.2 Taxation

The growth in taxation can be used as an alternative indicator of increased government involvement in market economies.

Taxation can be held to impose three kinds of burden on people. The first of these is the idea that in order to pay tax people have to fill in forms, keep records of income and expenditure, write letters to the Inland Revenue and so on. Costs of this kind to households and firms are called **compliance costs**.

The second cost of taxation is the effect of the tax itself on incomes. Paying tax reduces people's money incomes and thus their ability to buy goods and services. Whether people are better or worse off, of course, depends on what the government does with the revenue it raises through taxation. Some people will be net gainers from the combined impact of taxation and government expenditure; others will be net losers. Consequently, we can think of the income loss of households from taxation in two ways: we can say that taxation reduces the money income of most taxpayers; or we can say that taxation and government expenditure together reduce the real income of some households.

The third cost imposed by taxation involves a more abstract idea. Consider the imposition by the government in its 1984 budget of VAT on hot take-away foods. Before the budget, people made their decisions regarding the sorts of food they wished to consume, trying to obtain as much satisfaction as they could from their incomes. After the budget, the prices of hot take-away foods rose relative to those of other foods as a result of the new tax. People who continued to buy the same amount of hot take-away food as before the budget clearly suffered an income loss. They were paying more money for the same quantity of goods. What, however, was the position of people who regarded hot food as too dear and switched from fish and chips to pork pies purchased from supermarkets? They too were made worse off by the new tax, even though they acted in such a way that they avoided paying it. They could be said to have lost simply because the tax changed existing relative prices and caused them to alter their choices. This notion is known as the *excess burden* of a tax. There are many examples of it. For instance, an increased income tax may lead a worker to work fewer hours of overtime; an increase in corporation tax may cause a firm to raise its prices and cut its production.

It is thus the idea of *interference with choice* which provides the principal justification for using taxation as an indicator of the importance of government in the economy. As our hot food example indicates, however, the amount of tax collected is not necessarily a good indicator of the impact of government. The more people change their behaviour as a result of the tax (that is, the less hot take-away food they consume), the less revenue the government collects from the tax, but the greater is the excess burden of the tax.

It can also be argued that governments can increase their impact on the economy without raising taxation. Thus, to the extent that governments run deficit budgets, government influence may be understated by looking at taxation alone.

In practical terms, looking at the *revenue* side of the government accounts in relation to a measure of national product provides at least as many problems as looking at the expenditure side. What, after all, is a tax? Do we include TV licence fees, national insurance contributions, prescription charges? None the less, taxation statistics do provide an alternative measure and can be used to chronicle the growth in the importance of government, as in Table 1.4.

Table 1.4 UK taxation revenue in relation to GDP at factor cost 1955–85

Year	Taxation revenue* (£ m.)	Tax as % of GDP
1955	5.7	33.7
1965	11.0	34.9
1975	38.5	40.2
1980	82.0	41.2
1982	106.9	45.4
1984	122.9	45.1
1985	134.6	44.5

* Taxation revenue includes income tax, taxes on expenditure, taxes on capital, rates and national insurance contributions.

Sources: Economic Trends; Financial Statistics

1.1.3 Employment

Given the problems associated with financial estimates of the importance of government in the economy, it seems an attractive idea to consider a *real* measure, giving a direct indication of the extent to which the public sector makes use of the country's resources. One such measure is to take the number of workers employed by government as a percentage of the total workforce in employment.

Alas, here too there are serious problems. One problem again involves the treatment of nationalised industries. It is usual in exercises of this kind to treat 'public corporations' separately from the rest of government employment. Another problem is that official figures do not normally distinguish between full-time and part-time workers. Since a significant amount of the increase in the size of government employment in the 1970s involved the hiring of part-time workers, such information is clearly relevant. In addition the statistics can be interpreted in two ways. A growth in government employment can be taken to indicate an aggressively expanding public sector, using resources which would otherwise have been available to the private sector; or to indicate a private sector declining quite independently of any government action, with the public sector expanding in an attempt to soak up increasing quantities of unused resources.

Table 1.5 indicates changes in public sector employment. It shows that combined central and local government employment has grown substantially since the 1950s, from 12.2 per cent of workers in employment in 1956 to 20.7 per cent in 1984. If we include the employment of public corporations, we can see that public sector

Table 1.5 UK public sector employment as percentage of total working population in employment 1956–84

Year	Central & local govt. employment*		Public corporations employment	
	Thousands	%	Thousands	%
1956	2,897	12.2	2,419	10.2
1960	3,040	12.5	2,200	9.1
1965	3,524	14.2	2,028	8.2
1970	4,092	16.8	2,025	8.3
1975	4,852	19.6	2,035	8.2
1980	4,995	20.0	2,038	8.2
1981	4,953	20.7	1,867	7.8
1982	4,912	20.8	1,756	7.4
1983	4,910	20.9	1,663	7.1
1984	4,893	20.7	1,611	6.8

Sources: UK National Accounts; National Income and Expenditure
* Excludes HM Forces.

employment stood at 27.5 per cent of the workforce in employment in 1983. It is interesting to note that although central and local government employment actually fell between 1980 and 1983, it did so at a slower rate than employment in the rest of the economy.

1.2 Attitudes to big government

Whatever the measurement problems, we can accept that governments have played a large and increasingly important role in the functioning of market economies. There are two prominent views regarding the desirability of government intervention in the economy.

1.2.1 Market optimists

Market optimists begin from economic theory which draws a picture of an ideal world of perfect competition. There are large numbers of small producers and consumers meeting together in markets to buy and sell. No participant in a market can have any influence over its behaviour. In this world, the resulting market prices lead to scarce resources being combined to produce as many as possible of the commodities which people want.

The goods exchanged in these markets are private goods; that is, they can only be consumed by one person or household and so people must compete for them in markets. The production of these goods is assumed to have no side-effects, either good or bad, on other producers or on consumers. Everyone has complete information about the quality of goods and factors of production for sale and of the prices ruling throughout the various markets. This information stretches to cover what is going to happen in these markets in the future. There are no costs involved in obtaining this information and no other costs from engaging in market transactions (for example, no transport costs).

All people are assumed to be the best judges of their own interests and to use market prices as signals to allow them, given the size of their incomes and the resources they possess, to make the consumption and production decisions which most advance their material well-being. Since the income at their disposal is obtained from selling factors required in production, people are rewarded for contributing as best they can to the production of goods desired by other people.

In such a world there are very strong incentives for people to work hard, to acquire skills, to save, to invest, and to economise in consumption. In such a world, markets always clear – that is, demand for each good always equals its supply at the equilibrium price. All markets are always in equilibrium. This includes the market for labour and it follows that unemployment does not exist. There is no role at all for government.

Everyone accepts that the real world is not and cannot be like this. Market optimists, however, set up such a model as an ideal standard against which the real world can be assessed. To the extent that there are deviations from the 'ideal' in practice, a role may be admitted for government to attempt to move things towards the 'ideal'. Each involvement of government in the market economy must be justified in these terms. A number of reasons are commonly accepted by market optimists for intervention in the economy.

A regulatory role for government

Government must have, at the very least, a role in regulating the market economy. Commodities are neither produced nor consumed instantaneously – production takes time, with labour hired and paid in advance of the sale of the product, and consumers place orders to be met at future dates. As a result many of the transactions in markets do not involve the direct provision of goods and services, but rather involve *contracts* to work, to pay, and to supply at future dates. Since market participants need to be confident that contracts will be carried out, a legal framework is essential. There must be clear rules about the ownership of property, and methods must exist for enforcing those rules. The very nature of a market system, based as it is on contracts and the private ownership of property, clearly requires a government to regulate it.

Public goods

Market optimists also accept the existence of goods other than private goods. At the other extreme are goods which are *not* diminished by being consumed by one person and hence remain available to be consumed by others (that is, they are non-competitive in consumption). One ship's use of the light from a lighthouse does not prevent other ships from using it. Such goods may be called public goods, collective goods or social goods.

These goods pose a problem because they are available even to those who have not paid for them. In economics jargon, this is known as the failure of the exclusion principle to operate. Those who attempt to benefit without paying are known as 'free riders'. In a large community many may attempt to act as free riders, hoping that others will pay for the provision of the public good, enabling them to enjoy the benefit 'free'. The net result may be that a good is not produced, even though everyone would like it to be. It is worth noting that if public goods are provided they cannot be rejected. Thus, an opponent of Cruise missiles may demonstrate against their installation, but as long as they remain part of the defence system, they are 'consumed' equally by everyone in the country.

Defence expenditure, indeed, is probably the most important practical example of public goods, though there are several others of significance. It is possible to imagine a public good being provided collectively by a small community. In our type of society, however, the only way in which most public goods are likely to be provided is through some sort of compulsory taxation and expenditure mechanism; that is, by means of a government of some kind. People at the dark end of a street are far more likely to complain to the council than to act voluntarily to improve the street lighting.

Social costs and benefits

The fact that the costs and benefits of provision often extend beyond those directly involved, is a further reason for the market optimist to accept government intervention.

Undertaking an extra course of training may increase a person's earning power – in this respect it confers a private benefit. However, it may be argued that, by adding to the economy's stock of skilled labour, it also bestows a *social benefit* on the whole community. Yet if people only take account of their own private interests in making consumption and investment decisions, this social benefit will be ignored. Less training may then take place than is socially desirable. Government encouragement of training, for example via subsidy, may be needed if the appropriate amount of training is to occur.

There are also the many examples of social costs which would not be taken into account if all decisions were left to the private market – for example, the smoking chimneys, and the inadequately tested pharmaceutical drugs. These are cases where goods and services would be provided in different amounts or by different processes if *all* the costs, not just the private ones to the individual producers, were considered. These questions are often dealt with in economics under the heading of *externalities* or of external costs and benefits. Many economists see here a clear argument for governments to intervene in the market to change the set of prices facing people when they make their decisions, so that the prices reflect all the benefits and costs associated with each act of production and consumption.

True market optimists are, however, likely to argue that many of these problems arise because of an inadequate definition of property rights. Thus, if everyone knew that the owner of a factory with a smoky chimney had the legal right to produce goods in any way, then a market could operate to establish the 'bribe' the residents would need to pay to persuade the factory owner to move elsewhere, to use a cleaner method of production or to cease production altogether. The only problems would be seen as being the size of the community (which may be too small to pay an acceptable bribe, or too large to organise effectively) and the fact that citizens have become unwilling to act voluntarily on a collective basis. In other words, people have become too dependent on governments in matters in which they could act for themselves through a market. Market optimists would probably add that governments in practice often permit producers to ignore social costs rather than force producers to take account of them. Governments, after all, allow producers of goods and services to dump nuclear waste at sea and to fly noisy aircraft in the early hours of the morning. Governments give themselves considerable freedom to ignore the wishes of consumers. These views of the 'true market optimists' considerably dilute their acceptance of the argument that the existence of social costs and benefits can only be 'corrected' by government intervention.

Characteristics of economic agents

As well as the goods being different from those in the world of perfect markets, the *participants* are different – there are large as well as small producers of goods and services; and they operate in markets with much less information than is assumed in our ideal model. Again the desire to correct such market imperfections can lead market optimists to propose government intervention.

However, many see the lack of competition in markets as a criticism not of the market system but of governments themselves, for allowing particular groups to establish positions of power in some markets. Attention is often focused on labour markets where it is argued that legislation favouring trade unions together with the social security system has reduced competition. Rather oddly, there seems far less concern about reduced competition in product markets.

On the lack of information in markets, the market optimist

usually admits that participants in actual markets do not have perfect information and that the acquisition of information requires time and resources. Thus, people will only seek to obtain information about market prospects up to a certain point. Beyond this, the improvement in trading prospects resulting from more information will be less than the cost of acquiring it. With incomplete information, some trading is bound to involve wrong decisions. In goods markets, for example, there will on some occasions be shortages, queues and waiting lists. On other occasions there will be gluts, and goods will be stored.

Although there may be an acceptance of the need for the government to help provide fuller information to market participants in order to improve decisions, there is no mandate for massive government intervention in this view. At most, governments may have a small role in important markets in helping to increase the available information, for example via job centres in labour markets. Market optimists might even argue that very often governments are worse informed about market prospects than the participants in the markets themselves!

Merit and demerit goods

Market optimists may accept some government intervention through believing that individuals are not always the best judges of their own welfare. They may believe, for example, that heroin users have not fully and rationally taken account of all the costs and benefits of their actions. They may therefore accept that there are some goods which the community should discourage or prevent individuals from consuming (demerit goods) and others it should encourage (merit goods) simply because the community may sometimes know better what is good for people than do individuals themselves. Even the most ardent of believers in the free market will usually turn out to be opposed to the widespread availability of pornographic films or hard drugs, thereby accepting the need for government regulation.

Income distribution

Finally, some market optimists may accept a limited role for government in the redistribution of income. However, they would argue that any change in the distribution of income produced by the market will interfere with incentives and reduce the efficiency of operation of the market. Thus, redistribution should be kept to a minimum.

1.2.2 The market pessimists

Market pessimists accept the arguments for government intervention in markets outlined above but see them as justifying *much more* government intervention than do market optimists. Essentially this is because they believe that governments, chosen as they are by a political process, are better able to know the needs and interests of the community as a whole than a market system driven by impersonal forces of supply and demand. The market system can also be seen as a voting process, but one where the number of votes people have increases with their incomes. Market pessimists prefer the one-person-one-vote of the political system. Despite the manifest shortcomings of all governments, they believe that the interaction of political and economic power will produce a wiser and fairer set of decisions than would economic power alone.

They would also apply social costs and benefits arguments much more widely. For example, they might argue for job subsidies on the basis that unemployment imposes external costs on the economy as a whole, in the form perhaps of increased crime rates and a lowering of community confidence. Market pessimists are, as well, very concerned about lack of competition in product markets, seeing this as an unavoidable outcome of the nature of production and of the structure of economic power. Some monopolies are regarded as being justified for industrial, commercial or social reasons. These monopolies, they argue, should be nationalised and run by the government on behalf of the whole community. In other cases, they see no justification for market power being concentrated in a few hands, preferring the government to oversee mergers and take-overs in the private sector, and to influence the way private firms act in relation to their employees, their customers, and the rest of the community.

Uncertainty and stabilisation

Rather than merely advocate government help in acquiring extra bits of information, market pessimists view market economies as being *characterised* by ignorance and uncertainty. Uncertainty inevitably generates waves of pessimism and optimism. In some periods those with money may be better advised to abstain from investing, keeping their money idle while they wait to see what will happen next. Resources (including labour) may then remain unused, rather than be used in ways which entrepreneurs fear will lead to losses. At other periods, entrepreneurs may be confident about the future and fall over themselves to acquire resources to use in production, bidding up prices in the process.

The market pessimist therefore views the market economy as being intrinsically unstable, moving from periods of low production and high unemployment to periods of high demand for goods and resources with great pressure on prices. This suggests that the government should operate a macroeconomic policy, spending more than it receives in taxation (budget deficit) in periods of recession, and saving on behalf of the economy (budget surplus) in periods of very high demand. In other words, the government should continually intervene in the market system to help the economy cope with uncertainty.

Income distribution

Market pessimists do not accept that unfettered markets produce a just distribution of income. They would argue that the existing income distribution depends not only on the operation of the market system but also upon the society's laws of inheritance, a matter on which perfectly competitive models are silent. They would further propose that the community should see itself as responsible for its individual members, and should not accept an income distribution determined by starting positions, ability and chance. A person's value to the community is not, they would suggest, determined merely by his or her contribution to production. Notions of fairness and equity are vital elements in a humane society.

1.3 Summary

We can summarise the possible arguments for government intervention which we have considered above in Table 1.6 (overleaf).

Further reading

The problems associated with the measurement of the size of the public sector are dealt with in some detail in Brown and Jackson (1982) Ch. 6. Discussions of particular issues especially of the 'relative price effect' can be found in Price (1979), Elliott and Fallick (1981), Gowland (1979), Heald (1983) and other sources.

Material on the growth of the importance of the public sector over the years is in Peacock and Wiseman (1967) and in many articles since then. Brown and Jackson (1982) provides a comprehensive set of references to public expenditure growth in a number

Table 1.6 Government intervention in the economy

Governmental role	Reason	Type of government action
1. Allocation of resources	Public goods; social costs and benefits; monopoly or monopsony; inadequate level of competition; lack of information and uncertainty; merit or demerit goods.	Laws governing actions of participants in markets; taxes and subsidies; nationalisation; providing additional information to market participants; increasing competition.
2. Stabilisation	Lack of information and uncertainty leading to under- or over-spending	Fiscal policy; monetary policy; incomes policy.
3. Distribution	Market imperfect; perfect market distribution unjust; actual distribution produced by laws unrelated to market incentives (e.g. laws of inheritance).	Taxes and transfers; changing laws influencing distribution; increasing competition in markets; incomes policies.

of countries. A good recent treatment of public expenditure and taxation developments at a very accessible level is found in Griffiths and Wall (1984) Chs 13 and 14. The role of government in the mixed economy is dealt with in most introductory economics texts and at a higher level in most public finance texts. Recommended introductory treatments include Grant and Shaw (1980) Ch. 1. At the higher level, Brown and Jackson (1982) Ch. 2 again provides much of what is needed.

Grant and Shaw (1980) also deals effectively with the topic of external costs and benefits as well as providing a variety of examples of them in various chapters of the book. The original source of much of the later discussion on property rights was an article by Coase (1960), reprinted in Breit and Hochmann (1971). This contains a number of entertaining examples of issues and is a good basis for discussion.

Many public expenditure and taxation issues are dealt with in various issues of the Treasury's monthly *Economic Progress Reports*.

Questions

*: Answers to these questions are discussed in Part II below.

1.* (a) Explain the 'mixed economy' approach to the allocation of scarce resources.

(b) What factors determine the extent to which an economy is mixed? (ACA, June 1982)

2.* Explain, with examples, the terms 'external costs' and 'external benefits'. Why and how might the government discourage activities involving excessive external costs? (London, Jan. 1984)

3. The market has been described as a good servant but a poor master. Explain what you think is meant by this statement and discuss whether or not other economic systems are superior to the market in your opinion. (JMB, June 1983)

4. Discuss the reasons for divergences between social and private costs and benefits. (Oxford, June 1977)

5.* What are the main differences between public and private goods? What factors should determine the charges made for school meals? (Oxford, June 1979)

Chapter two
Taxation issues

We can now look at the purpose of taxation. In addition, we can consider in more detail the question raised in Chapter 1 concerning taxation and incentives.

2.1 The purpose of taxation

We can begin with the proposition that tax has to be collected to pay for the government expenditure which the community wants. But this begs several questions, and two in particular: (1) how do we determine the desired level of government expenditure? and (2) who should actually pay the taxes required to fund that expenditure?

2.1.1 The benefit principle

We could perhaps hope to discover a principle which would both indicate to government what its level of expenditure should be and solve the problem of how much each household in the economy should play towards that expenditure. This is the notion encompassed by the **benefit principle** – that each household should pay tax equal to the benefit it receives from government expenditure. Written down like this the benefit principle seems a perfectly fair and reasonable idea. However, it runs into one of the problems which we discussed in Chapter 1, namely the free rider problem in the provision of public goods. In the case of private goods, each household declares the benefit it is receiving from goods through the prices it is prepared to pay for them. But with public goods, remember, a market price cannot be established in the same way because non-payers as well as payers can freely consume the goods once they have been provided.

Benefit derived from a commodity is subjective and differs from one household to another. It follows that if people are not required to declare through a market the benefit they receive from the consumption of goods, we have no basis under the benefit principle for determining how much each taxpayer should contribute towards the provision of public goods. We could, it is true, ask households how much benefit they are obtaining from public goods, but we would only expect honest answers from the naïve, the dim-witted and the morally pure.

It would be possible to respond to this by saying that public goods are not really very important outside textbooks. This, though, would be to ignore the fact that the public goods example is only an extreme form of the very large and inescapable problem of interdependence in society – that is, that many of the economic actions of individuals affect the level of well-being of others in the economy. In all such cases of interdependence, whether public goods or otherwise, there is no economic mechanism for measuring how much other people are advantaged or disadvantaged. For instance, as with public goods, there can be no objective answer to the question of how much governments should spend on the provision of merit goods or on discouraging the consumption of demerit goods. Equally it cannot be completely clear who benefits from such expenditure nor to what degree. For a variety of reasons, then, the benefit principle as a guide to government taxation policy falls flat.

All that remains of the benefit principle is the idea that governments should only spend if that expenditure benefits people and people should only pay tax to the extent that they benefit. With no means of assessing *individual* benefit the principle then reduces to an advocacy of *aggregate* expenditure equal to *aggregate* taxation – that is, a balanced budget.

We can perhaps go a little further in theory and say that governments should only continue to spend if the benefits people obtain through paying the last pound of taxation are at least equal to the benefits they could obtain from using that pound in some other way. According to this view, if people would rather pay less tax, preferring, for example, to have bigger cars and smaller roads, then government expenditure is too large. We have, however, no way of measuring people's relative valuations of public and private expenditure other than through very imprecise political mechanisms, such as general elections where a voter has only one vote but may have a variety of opinions about many issues, one of which is the level of government expenditure.

2.1.2 Ability to pay

If the benefit principle is of little help to policy-making, what else can we try? One step is to try to make the question easier by splitting it into two stages. We can put to one side the problem of the level of public expenditure. Then we can say: *given* that we wish public expenditure to be £x billion, how much should different people be taxed in order to pay for it?

This enables us to concentrate on another major purpose of taxation: the achievement of greater equality than might result from an uncontrolled market economy. The case for the transfer of income from rich to poor can be seen as an important example of the argument about social costs and benefits. Society as a whole may gain as a result of a more equal distribution of income for many possible reasons. For example, it may provide greater equality of opportunity, thereby allowing the society to make greater use of its stock of talent. Again, greater income equality may lead to lower rates of infant mortality and to lower crime rates. Or greater equality may simply accord better with the social conscience than a situation in which poverty manifestly coexists with plenty.

As well as wishing to transfer income from rich to poor in the interests of **vertical** equity, governments may also be interested in **horizontal** transfers (that is, transfers among groups of people for reasons other than equalising income). The most common form of horizontal income tranfer is from young to old through the provision of state pensions which are paid to rich and poor alike. Any transfer, whether vertical or horizontal, requires the government to decide precisely what the aim of the transfer is and the desired extent of the transfer. In practice, there is much confusion in government transfer policies and it is quite common for some government transfer schemes to be in conflict with others.

If we concentrate on the question of **vertical** equity, we can distinguish a number of possible approaches:

1. We could say that we wished to establish a floor to income at a level which we would regard as the minimum necessary for a tolerable existence. Our aim would be to allow no people to fall below this level, irrespective of their ability, character and behaviour. It would not be easy to decide upon the minimum income levels for different family sizes, but it would be clear that we were not interested in the question of equality among people whose unsupported incomes were above the minimum level.

2. Another approach could be to distinguish factors which were associated with hardship in society. We might decide that the most important such factors were unemployment, large families, single-parent families, illness, and old age. We would then design a series of payments for people in these groups. Since our principal concern would be with hardship, payments would need to be means-tested; that is, they would only be made available to people whose unsupported incomes were below some figure and they would be graded so that people on lower incomes received more benefits. Means-testing of benefits poses problems, but not to means-test them could result in horizontal transfers taking place as well as vertical ones. Indeed, one may find such things as young people paying taxes in order to provide pensions for better off old people.

3. Yet another possibility would be to attempt to make incomes more equal over the whole range of incomes, without paying attention to the particular circumstances of individuals or households. Thus we might have a *progressive* income tax structure which acts so that people on higher incomes pay a larger proportion of their incomes to the tax collector.

The problems of achieving these different types of vertical equity would be mainly ones of determining precise objectives and of administration, were it not for a major complicating factor. This is the argument that redistributing income vertically is likely to damage incentives and hence interfere with the efficiency of the economy. This view rests on two major propositions:

1. That people are principally motivated by the desire for material gain;

2. That the market rewards people in line with their productivity (that is, in line with their contribution to the production of commodities which people in the economy want).

Both of these propositions may be disputed, but they are widely held to be true and so it is usual to regard the two aims of *equity* and *efficiency* to be in conflict. The standard metaphor is that cutting the cake into more equal slices will lead to a smaller cake.

The incentives usually discussed are the incentives which people have to work, to save, and to take risks. By far the most attention, however, has been paid to the question of the extent to which higher taxes lead to reductions in the amount of market work people are willing to undertake. Let us consider this question.

2.2 Income tax changes and labour supply

The labour supply question is normally framed in terms of the number of hours of work a worker will offer to the labour market at different wage rates. It is accepted that once workers are in jobs, they may seem to have relatively little control over the length of their working week. However, it is argued that we only choose a week as the period to consider for our convenience. If we were to consider a longer period of time (perhaps as long as the worker's lifetime) we would see that there are quite a few ways in which workers can vary how much work they do – through length of holidays, working at more than one job at a time, age of retirement, taking unpaid leave and so on.

It is further contended that the length of the working week (or working year etc.) may strongly influence the decision which a worker makes to accept or reject a particular job. Thus, a worker may be required to work a certain amount of overtime each week, but may have chosen that job knowing that overtime working was expected. Nevertheless we may still be sceptical about this whole issue since the form of analysis we are using here (marginal analysis) implies that workers are able to make small adjustments to the amount of work they do in response to changes in wage rates.

Having accepted a marginal framework for our analysis, we next need to assume that workers base their labour supply decisions on their real (net-of-tax) wage rate, that is the purchasing power of an hour's work after subtracting income tax. In other words, by linking labour supply to the real wage rate we are assuming that the only reason that people work is to enable them to buy goods and services. One implication of this is that time can be divided into two categories – work (by which we mean paid jobs) and non-work. It is usual to refer to all non-work as 'leisure', though it is true that people spend significant amounts of time engaged in activities which are neither work nor leisure (for example, doing housework, travelling to work, and reading books like this one).

The part played by taxation in the labour supply decision can now be investigated. A reduction in the rate of income tax is equivalent to a wage rise, since both enable workers to buy more goods in return for the same amount of work as before. 'Leisure' has become more expensive, since any hour of non-work is at the cost of more goods forgone. We might therefore expect that the tax cut would lead to workers giving up some of the now more expensive 'leisure' (that is, working more hours in a paid job). This is the 'substitution effect' – the substitution of work for leisure because of the change in their relative price.

However, as a result of the tax cut, any given expenditure of effort on work now yields more goods and services. This extra real income from the tax cut is termed the 'income effect'. Higher income can of course be spent entirely on consuming the extra goods and services now available, or it may be used in part to purchase more leisure (that is, to work less). The income tax cut, then, produces an 'income effect' leading to fewer hours being worked.

We can see that the substitution effect has resulted from the fact that the worker's *marginal* rate of taxation has fallen, changing the relationship between an extra hour of work and an extra hour of 'leisure'. The income effect has arisen because the *average* rate of taxation has fallen, changing the total quantity of goods available to the worker from a given amount of work. The substitution effect leads to an increase in the number of hours worked; the income effect leads to a reduction. What will the outcome be?

Unfortunately, on theoretical grounds we have no way of knowing. The answer will be different for different individuals depending on the way in which they value goods and 'leisure'. We have two extreme possibilities. The worker: (a) takes all gains in the form of extra goods and considerably reduces 'leisure' hours; (b) takes all gains in the form of extra hours of 'leisure' and continues to consume the same amount of goods as before the tax cut. In between the two extremes there are many possibilities, some of which involve fewer hours of work than before the tax cut. Others involve more.

We can summarise all this in two diagrams. In Fig. 2.1 we place income (representing purchasing power) on the vertical axis and 'leisure' on the horizontal axis. Since the number of hours of 'leisure' possible in a week is fixed at 168 hours, the number of hours a worker wishes to work will be 168 hours minus the amount of leisure taken.

We can then construct an indifference map, $(U_1, U_2, $ etc.) showing the way in which the worker values goods and 'leisure' with each indifference curve representing the combinations of income and 'leisure' which yield a particular level of satisfaction. The shape of the curves simply illustrates the principle of diminishing marginal utility. As income (goods) increases along a curve (and leisure decreases), workers become progressively less willing to sacrifice 'leisure' for income (goods). Thus the curves are steep at their left-hand end where income is high, and relatively flat at

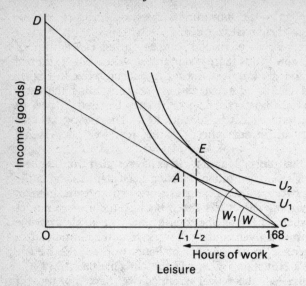

Fig. 2.1 Impact on labour supply of a fall in tax rates

their right-hand end where the worker has a great deal of 'leisure' and a low income. Next, we add a budget line (BC) which expresses the net hourly wage rate (after tax). It does this by showing the amount of income a worker could receive at the existing wage rate by giving up varying amounts of 'leisure'. Given these possibilities, a person will attempt to achieve the combination of income and 'leisure' which will give the greatest amount of total satisfaction. This is shown at point A, because A is the point along BC which is on the highest indifference curve.

Next we assume that the tax rate is cut, so that for any number of hours worked more income can now be obtained. The budget line swings up to CD. Our worker is able to move to a higher level of satisfaction (point E on U_2). In our diagram, this involves fewer hours of work (the number of hours of 'leisure' rises from L_1 to L_2). In this case the income effect, with its tendency to increase the consumption of 'leisure', outweighs the substitution effect which acts to reduce the consumption of 'leisure'. However, it is also possible to draw the diagram so that more hours of work result. Everything depends on the exact shape of the indifference curves and on the wage rates and tax cuts involved.

It is usual to assume that people on low wage rates will respond to a tax cut by offering to work longer hours, with the substitution effect being stronger than the income effect, but that the result of the tax cut becomes less certain when we consider workers on higher rates of pay. At some high rate of pay, it is accepted that for most workers, the income effect becomes stronger than the substitution effect and workers will offer fewer hours of work as taxes fall, as in Fig. 2.1. This can be shown by a labour supply curve which can be constructed from Fig. 2.1. In Fig. 2.2 we have wage rate on the vertical axis (not income as in Fig. 2.1) and hours of work supplied on the horizontal axis. At a wage rate above a certain level (w_1), we have a backward bending supply curve, with the income effect outweighing the substitution effect.

This analysis of the individual labour supply decision can be made much more complex. We can, for example, assume that the worker has income other than that which he receives from a job. We can deal with more complicated tax schedules with increasing marginal tax rates; with wage rates which change depending on the number of hours worked; with the existence of unemployment benefits; with the cost of transport to work and so on. We can analyse decisions of whole households as well as those of individuals.

However, none of these refinements alters the basic conclusion that we cannot predict from theory how any particular worker will respond to a cut in the rate of income tax.

What then can we do? We know that the issue is an important one since several governments (including those presently of the USA and UK) have argued that income tax cuts will encourage

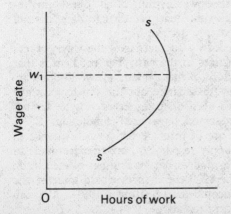

Fig. 2.2 A backward-bending labour supply curve

people to work harder and longer, with the implication that this will benefit the economy. It may be helpful to examine how people respond in practice to a reduction in taxation.

Two methods have been extensively tried – the use of questionnaires and econometric testing. The questionnaire approach asks workers how a change in tax rate (or net wage rate) would be likely to affect the amount of work they do; but it tries to eliminate the impact of preconceived ideas by the way the questions are framed and the order in which they are asked. Information is sought about the likely behaviour of workers in such a way that workers do not know the central purpose of the questionnaire. This is very difficult to do and the results of all research based upon this approach have been criticised.

Perhaps the best known survey of this type among high income earners in the UK is that carried out by Break in 1956 among a sample of accountants and lawyers. He concluded that only a small number of persons experienced net tax effects, with the disincentive effect being not significantly greater than the incentive effect. However, in a similar study in 1969, Fields and Stanbury found significant *disincentive* effects of taxation. But particular criticisms have been made of the Fields and Stanbury study and its conclusions have been called into doubt. The most thorough interview study of low income workers in the UK has been that of Brown and Levin, published in 1974. They enquired into the impact of taxation on attitudes to overtime among 2000 weekly paid workers and concluded that, if anything, taxation had led to a small *increase* in the amount of overtime worked. In summary, one can say that to the extent that it shows anything at all, questionnaire-based research favours the view that tax changes are not an important factor in labour supply decisions.

Econometric testing is based on an analysis of the way workers have responded to wage changes in the past. The problem is that many things will have influeced the amount of work done by people. It is not at all easy to separate out the impact of wage changes. Many studies have been done, especially in the United States, but the answers obtained have been conflicting. C. V. Brown attempted to make use of recent econometric evidence to analyse the likely labour supply response to tax changes made in the 1979 UK budget. He concluded that his findings offered 'little support to the view that the 1979 tax changes would increase the incentive to work at all income levels' (Brown 1983). All such conclusions are, however, very tentative.

A few attempts have been made to look at the impact of tax at a macroeconomic level. The American economist, Laffer, introduced the theoretical idea which became known as the Laffer curve. This suggested that at some high rate of tax, disincentive effects would become so strong that a further *increase* in tax rate would actually lead to a *fall* in tax revenue. This was an important idea in the early days of Reaganomics in the early 1980s but its practical relevance has never been shown. The few attempts which have been made to produce a Laffer curve for a real economy (for example by Beenstock (1979) in Britain) have been met with a great deal of scepticism. Other studies which have attempted to link tax rates in different countries with indicators of the economic performance of those countries have also been inconclusive.

Little more can be said except to point out that research can do little to assess whether people work harder (as distinct from longer) and whether the level of taxation affects people's willingness to seek promotion or undergo further training. Further, analysis of labour *supply* decisions does not address at all the possibility that someone willing to supply labour to the market will be unable to do so because of lack of demand in the economy. Total concentration on incentives and on the supply side of the economy derives from the assumption (considered in sect. 7.4) that the economy is at full employment and that any recorded unemployment is, in some sense, voluntary.

2.2.1 Other aspects of incentives

We have concentrated on one important argument regarding the impact of changes in government policy on incentives within an economy. Several other issues can also be considered using the same analytical framework based upon income and substitution effects. These include the effect of subsidising public transport fares on work effort and the impact of unemployment benefits on unemployment levels. The second of these is particularly controversial. Most recent writing has concluded that the level of unemployment benefits has had little effect on unemployment levels in the UK. However, Patrick Minford from the University of Liverpool and a few others have continued to argue vigorously that a strong link exists between these two variables.

Research on the impact of tax on incentives to save and to take risks has also led to no firm conclusions. The most we can say about this whole area is that claims by governments that their policies will release *large* amounts of effort and initiative should be treated with great wariness.

2.3 Choosing the best type of tax

So far we have been talking in terms of income tax only. However, there are many types of tax and one of the central concerns of public finance is to determine which kinds of tax are best. From our earlier discussion, we can say that we can compare different taxes in terms of:

1. their impacts on resource allocation;
2. their impacts on income distribution;
3. the costs involved in the collection of the taxes.

Under this last heading we include compliance costs, that is, the costs borne by taxpayers in meeting the demands of the tax collectors. It is also possible that different taxes have different macroeconomic impacts (for example, on the rate of inflation) which governments may wish to take into account. Rather than deal with specific types of tax here, we shall consider one debate which has been of considerable political as well as economic interest.

2.3.1 Direct and indirect taxes

Direct taxes can be most easily thought of as being the type of tax where the tax payable depends on the circumstances of each taxpayer. Thus, two people doing the same job and being paid the same wage may pay different amounts of tax because one receives income from some other source also, has a tax allowance for mortgage interest payments or has dependent parents. Income tax, a direct tax, is by some margin the most important single tax in the UK as Table 2.1 shows.

Indirect taxes are taxes on items, and the person responsible for handing over the tax to the government may not bear the final burden of the tax. For example, an increase in the tax on beer is likely to be felt mainly by beer-drinkers in the form of higher beer

Table 2.1 Structure of taxation in the UK, 1985

Revenues from different tax bases as percentage of total tax revenue

Income tax	NI. Contributions	Rates	Taxes on expenditure	Taxes on capital
39.3	16.2	10.2	32.6	1.6

Source: Financial Statistics

prices, even though the extra tax will be paid to the government by the brewing companies. If the increased tax is passed on in the form of a higher price for beer, each person buying a pint of beer will pay the same tax. The tax paid will not (as in the direct tax case) depend on the circumstances or the income of the taxpayer. The most important indirect taxes in the UK are VAT and excise taxes on petrol, motor cars, cigarettes and alcoholic drinks.

It is worth noting that very often the differences between particular indirect taxes (for example, between VAT and the purchase tax which it replaced) or between particular direct taxes (for example, between income tax and national insurance contributions) will be more important than the differences between indirect taxes as a whole and direct taxes. So, indeed, may be the way in which a particular tax is organised and administered (for example, whether the present VAT system in which the standard rate of tax is 15 per cent but some goods are zero-rated is retained or whether many goods now zero-rated will be taxed at the higher rate). However, since most debate has been over direct and indirect taxes as a whole, we shall concentrate on them.

2.3.2 Impacts on resource allocation

Do direct and indirect taxes have different impacts on incentives? There is no logical reason why they should have. People should take account of the total taxes they are paying. The central issue, after all, is the quantity of goods people can obtain in exchange for a given amount of work. Both direct and indirect taxes will affect this exchange.

It is possible to argue, however, that a variety of different taxes should be used to raise tax revenue and that it is therefore desirable to maintain a sensible balance between direct and indirect taxes. This argument depends upon the idea that the income effect (depending as it does on the average rate of taxation) will be unchanged no matter how taxation revenue is raised, but that the substitution effect (which leads to the discouragement of work effect) will be less if tax revenue is raised from a variety of sources. Suppose we were to have only an income tax. In order to collect the required amount of taxation and to have some income redistribution in the tax system, the marginal rate of tax for some taxpayers may have to be very high. If we were to have a variety of taxes, less revenue would need to be raised from each type of tax, so that the marginal rates required for each tax would be correspondingly lower.

Government and the economy

Let us take a simple example. Consider the case of people earning £20,500 a year before tax and spending all post-tax income on goods (that is, we are ignoring for the moment the problem of the effects of different taxes on saving). Assume we initially only have income tax, levied at the following marginal rates:

Annual income band	Marginal tax rate (%)
0–£10,000	30
£10,001–£15,000	40
£15,001–£18,000	50
£18,001–£21,000	60

Since these are marginal tax rates, our taxpayers will pay 30 per cent of their first £10,000 of incomes in tax; 40 per cent of their next £5,000; 50 per cent of their next £3,000; and 60 per cent of their final £2,500 of their incomes of £20,500. This comes to a total of £8,000 in tax, leaving a post-tax income of £12,500. This, we are assuming, will be spent entirely on goods.

Now the government alters the income tax bands to reduce income tax payments, and introduces a new 10 per cent indirect tax on all goods. We assume that the new tax is completely and immediately passed on in the form of higher prices.

The income tax bands are now as follows:

Annual income band	Marginal tax rate (%)
£0–£2,000	0
£2,001–£12,000	30
£12,001–£17,000	40
£17,001–£21,000	50

Our taxpayers pay £6,750 in income tax under this new scale, leaving £13,750 to be spent on goods. However, because of the 10 per cent goods tax, the goods which previously cost £12,500 now cost £13,750. The taxpayers are in total neither better off nor worse off. The same is true of the government which still collects £8,000 in tax from each of these taxpayers.

But, consider the *marginal* position. Assume that our taxpayers on £20,500 annual income are paid at a rate of £10 per hour. Prior, then, to the tax change, an extra hour of work would have netted them £4 worth of goods (the marginal rate of tax, remember, was 60 per cent). As we assume the new tax on goods to be fully passed on, goods which previously cost £4 will now cost £4.40. However, under the altered tax system, the marginal rate of tax for our taxpayers has fallen to 50 per cent and so they will now receive £5 net for an extra hour of work. It is clear that an additional hour of work will buy more goods for our taxpayers than previously. The income effect of taxation on them has not changed, *but the substitution effect has*. The cost of an extra hour of leisure in terms of income or goods forgone has risen, so that there is a greater incentive than before for the employee to work extra hours.

There are several difficulties with such simplistic examples:

1. For many workers there will be no change in the substitution effect, that is, no change in the marginal 'price' of work and leisure. A glance at our hypothetical tax schedules shows that for many workers (for example anyone earning between £2,000 and £10,000) the marginal rate of tax has *not* changed.

2. Remember, too, that there is little compelling evidence that taxation has a major effect on hours worked. Recall, for instance, the studies mentioned in section 2.2 above of Break and of Brown and Levin. Even where there is a substitution effect but no income effect, the impact may, in many cases, not be very great.

3. In addition, such a tax change would be accompanied inevitably by a considerable redistribution of income. In our example such a redistribution occurs with taxpayers earning £4,000 a year being £320 a year better off, while those on £15,000 a year are £200 a year worse off. In practice, it is impossible to separate the issues of incentives and income distribution. Any tax change will cause some people to be better off and others to be worse off.

4. It is also, at least theoretically, possible for taxation to alter the incentives to save and consume. Often it is suggested that indirect taxation is preferable because direct taxation taxes savings twice and therefore discourages saving in the economy. The idea is simply that as well as income being taxed, the interest which people receive on their savings from that income is also taxed. Proponents of this argument often go on to suggest that the UK's economic problems stem partly from savings being too low. The problem is that the argument is really one about the particular nature of the UK tax system. A direct tax system *can* be designed which does not involve the double taxation of savings. An expenditure tax is a direct tax of this kind.

2.3.3 Impacts on income distribution

It is usually suggested that direct taxes are more progressive (that is, they involve a greater redistribution of income from rich to poor) than indirect taxes.

There is confusion here too, since direct taxes need not be progressive. Indeed, the employee's national insurance contribution (which is a direct tax) has quite a regressive effect above middle incomes. The employee's contribution from October 1985 is as follows:

Earnings (£ per week)	Per cent payable on all earnings
35.50–55	5
55–90	7
90–265	9

The existence of the upper earnings limit of £265 per week means that people earning more than this amount pay less than 9 per cent of their earnings into the National Insurance Fund. Thus, an employee on the upper limit of £265 per week (£13,780 per year) pays £23.85 per week national insurance (that is, 9 per cent of earnings). But someone receiving £400 per week (£20,800 per year) will still pay £23.85 per week but this will now represent only approximately 6 per cent of earnings (a smaller proportion, notice, than people who are receiving between £55 and £90 per week).

Equally, indirect taxes can be made progressive through such devices as the levying of higher rates of tax on goods consumed principally by those on higher incomes. All that can be said is that, as they are operated in practice, most forms of direct tax are more progressive than most forms of indirect tax. Table 2.2 shows that in the UK direct taxes are progressive overall whereas indirect taxes are regressive.

If governments do wish to redistribute income by a considerable amount, however, it may well make things politically easier if part of the objective can be achieved by changing the balance among taxes. For instance, a government interested in improving the post-tax position of those on higher incomes at the expense of the worse off may be able to move in this direction by raising indirect taxes and lowering direct taxes. If the basic direct tax rate is taken to be the main indicator of tax policy (as seems to have been the case in the past) most taxpayers may believe they are better off, whereas many people on lower incomes may actually be paying more tax than before.

Table 2.2 Impact of direct and indirect taxes, UK, 1983

Direct and indirect tax as a percentage of gross household income by decile groups (ranked by original income)

Decile group	Gross household	Direct taxes (%)	Indirect taxes (%)	Total taxes (%)
Lowest	3,218	0.1	27.4	27.4
Second	3,065	0.5	26.0	26.5
Third	3,962	3.8	27.8	31.6
Fourth	5,711	11.8	25.4	37.2
Fifth	7,210	17.0	23.7	40.8
Sixth	8,748	18.2	22.7	40.9
Seventh	10,290	20.2	20.7	40.9
Eighth	12,311	21.1	19.7	40.8
Ninth	15,149	22.3	19.1	41.4
Highest	23,339	24.2	16.6	40.8

* Gross household income includes government cash benefits.
Source: Economic Trends, Dec. 1984

2.3.4 Administration and compliance

Yet again no general rules are possible here. VAT is widely agreed to have relatively high costs of collection and very high compliance costs, though, as a proportion of revenue raised from the tax, these declined considerably after 1979. This was largely as a result of the increase in the standard rate of VAT to 15 per cent which considerably increased the revenue raised at very little extra cost. Thus, a study by Sandford *et al.* (1981) estimated that in 1977–78 each one pound of revenue raised from VAT had cost the government 2.0 pence to collect and had involved compliance costs of 9.3 pence. By 1980–81 the administrative costs had fallen to 1.2 pence and the compliance costs to 5.1 pence for each pound of revenue raised. The compliance cost remains high in comparison with other taxes and is still a worry. Thus, a government study, *Burdens on Business* (1985), reported that 39 per cent of a sample of small businesses had mentioned VAT as a particular burden. However, it is clear that the costs of administering and of complying with a particular tax depend very much on the rates and the structure of the tax. The costs associated with VAT, for instance, would be much reduced if the threshold of annual turnover for VAT registration was considerably raised. Perhaps as many as 800,000 small businesses would be relieved of the burden of VAT if the threshold of £19,500 applicable in 1985 were raised to £50,000.

In any case, these arguments about costs can only be against VAT as a form of indirect tax not against indirect taxes in general. Some forms of indirect tax are easy and cheap to collect. In some developing countries, indeed, it is this factor which leads governments to be heavily dependent for revenue on indirect taxes, such as tariffs on imports.

2.3.5 Other arguments

There are other arguments for and against each type of tax. It is probably the case that increases in indirect tax will be passed on in the form of higher prices to a greater extent than will increases in direct tax. Thus, indirect taxes may be more inflationary, though this depends on the impact of tax changes on subsequent wage claims. The difference may not, especially in the longer run, be very great. Whether it is important depends on the policy objectives of government.

Also, indirect taxes are advantageous to exporters since international trade agreements allow a country to refund indirect taxes paid on exported goods. Direct taxes cannot be so refunded because their influence on final costs of production cannot easily be calculated. It can therefore be argued that exporters in countries with high indirect taxes and low direct taxes have an advantage in trade over those from countries with high direct and low indirect taxes. But there is little knowledge as to how quantitatively important this advantage is.

Finally, it has sometimes been claimed that indirect taxes allow more freedom because people can choose to avoid paying them by altering their spending and savings patterns. This is an obvious fallacy. It would be true if indirect taxes were levied on only a few goods. Then, for instance, people might avoid paying a tax on petrol by not driving a car. However, if indirect taxes are to contribute in a major way to government revenue, they must be on a wide range of goods and services and must be such that they can be no more easily avoided than income taxes. In any case, as we have shown earlier, if a tax does lead to people 'exercising choice' in such a way that they do not pay the tax, they still suffer a burden from the existence of the tax.

2.3.6 Conclusion

This all leads us to say that there are no strong arguments for direct taxes as a group or indeed for indirect taxes. At most, a case may be made out for maintaining some sort of balance between them, but no guidance is forthcoming from economic theory about the nature of that balance. Very often, debates about direct versus indirect taxes are cloaks behind which lies the politically sensitive issue of income redistribution.

Further reading

A compact but detailed explanation of the principal UK taxes is to be found in Jackson (1982). The theoretical approaches to taxation, including the benefit and ability to pay principles is thoroughly treated in Brown and Jackson (1982). Kay and King (1983) deals very well with all aspects of the British tax system, even managing to be entertaining from time to time. Brown and Jackson (1982) is to be particularly recommended for its treatment of the impact of taxation on the supply of labour. Brown (1983) provides more detail and explains well the problems associated with empirical work in this area. The attempt to estimate a Laffer curve for the UK is in Beenstock (1979) but this needs to be read critically. It is also advisable to consult the replies to Beenstock's article in the *Lloyds Bank Reviews* of Jan. and Apr. 1980.

The debate over unemployment benefits and the level of unemployment is summarised by Atkinson in Creedy (1981).

A useful treatment of the direct versus indirect tax question is in Griffiths and Wall (1984) Ch. 14. For more detail, consult Kay and King (1983). The study on the administrative and compliance costs of VAT is reported in Sandford *et al.* (1981) and the updating of this study is reported in Sandford (1984). Chapter 2 of Millward *et al.* (1983) surveys the primary literature on taxation and incentives and includes material on taxation and business decisions which we have not been able to deal with here. At a simpler level, Sandford's chapter in Grant and Shaw (1980) is to be recommended.

Questions

*: Answers to these questions are discussed in Part II below.

1.* Discuss the case for shifting the balance of taxation away from direct taxes to indirect taxes. (London, June 1984)

2.* Discuss the effects that an increase in social security payments might have on the level of unemployment. (London, June 1979)

3.* Discuss the main objectives of taxation, illustrating your answer with reference to the UK's system of taxation. (AEB, June 1985)

4. Explain the functions of taxation. What factors are likely to influence the rate of personal income tax imposed by the government? (JMB, June 1981)

5. Identify the objectives of government taxation and illustrate how these may be achieved by levying: (a) income tax; and (b) a tax on alcohol. (ICMA, May 1984)

Chapter three
Government production

In Chapter 1 we outlined six arguments for government intervention in the market economy. Such intervention may affect production in many ways. For example, governments may:

(a) tax citizens and use the proceeds to provide commodities produced by the private sector;
(b) subsidise private firms or give tax allowances to them;
(c) legislate to control the behaviour of private firms towards their customers, their workforces or the government;
(d) invest in the infrastructure of the economy (for instance, in transport networks, communications, housing or education);
(e) employ labour themselves to produce commodities which may be sold or distributed without charge to the public.

The last of these possibilities raises the question of the extent to which governments should be producers. In most economies government production is an important element in total product. The best simple indicator of this is government employment. In the UK in 1983, total government employment (including local authority and public corporation employment but excluding the armed forces) was 6.57 million and made up 28 per cent of the total working population in employment. In considering arguments about government production, we can usefully classify it under four headings.

3.1 Types of government production

3.1.1 Public administration

Government employment would exist even in an economy completely oriented towards private enterprise – to administer and enforce laws, to collect taxes and to disburse funds to private firms providing goods and services to the government.

3.1.2 Non-marketable commodities

Governments produce goods and services which *by their nature* cannot be sold in markets. This may be because of the 'free rider' problem discussed in Chapter 1 (as with national defence or police protection of citizens) or because the cost of collecting payment from users would be too high. Examples of this include footpaths and most roads and bridges. In some cases, however, although the *financing* of production is through taxation, the commodities are produced by private companies. This is done by private firms competing for government contracts to provide goods or to provide services for a specified period of time. Thus, the Navy's ships may be built in privately owned shipyards, roads may be constructed or repaired by private engineering firms and so on.

3.1.3 Marketable but non-marketed commodities

Many governments choose to produce and distribute commodities which could be marketed but finance them instead mainly through taxation. Sometimes charges are levied, such as prescription fees, but these charges are not clearly related to the value of the product received. Examples include motorways, police protection of property and the provision of health and education services. Often, such commodities are provided by both the public sector and the private sector as with public and private hospitals and schools. Sometimes part of a service will be produced by the public sector and part by the private sector. Such a case is the contracting-out to the private sector of the cleaning of public hospitals.

3.1.4 Marketed goods

Some commodities produced by the public sector are sold to the public. This is principally the area of production covered by the *nationalised industries*, though other public corporations also produce and market goods, as do firms which are partly private- and partly government-owned.

Council housing is an important area of production which straddles our last two classes. Payment is made for the product but the issues raised have more in common with those raised by government production of health and education services than by nationalised industries.

3.2 Areas of debate

Three issues, all of which concern the comparative merits of public and private sector production, have arisen. They are quite distinct, although the term *privatisation* has often been used in connection with all three.

3.2.1 Contracting-out

The central government and local authorities let out contracts to firms to build council houses and government buildings, to carry out road works, to provide defence equipment and so on. The present debate is over the extent to which this contracting system should be extended to other areas of government provision of services, in particular to things such as the cleaning of public hospitals, the supplying of hospital food and the collection of household refuse. The private sector can perform such functions. The question is whether the private sector is likely to carry them out better and/or more cheaply than the public sector.

3.2.2 The balance of mixed provision

We could argue for the provision of services such as education, health and housing entirely by the public secator or entirely by the private sector. In practice, though, the point of dispute centres on whether the balance of provision should be shifted away from the public sector towards the private sector. Examples include encouraging the construction of private hospitals and the purchase of private health insurance while limiting the growth of the National Health Service and the sale of council houses and the encouragement of private home ownership.

3.2.3 De-nationalisation

The form of this question has changed in recent years. We used to ask why certain industries (and not others) should have been taken into public ownership. Now we ask whether some (or all) of the nationalised industries should be sold off to the private sector. A subsidiary question is whether government shareholdings in private companies should be sold.

3.3 The arguments

3.3.1 The general case

The general case for private production rests on the ideas that:

(a) the profit motive, by encouraging firms to produce efficiently, leads to the provision of goods and services at low cost in terms of resources; *and*

(b) competition ensures that firms supply the type and quality of commodities that consumers want and keeps prices to consumers down.

Point (a) implies that people are principally motivated by the desire for material gain. This is widely assumed to be true although there is very little evidence to support it, as we saw in Chapter 2 when we considered the relationship between taxation and the incentive to work. Also implied here is the idea that firms always seek to maximise profits. However, many economists see the motivation of the firm as much more complex. Thus firms may '*satisfice*' rather than maximise – that is, they may seek only to make sufficient profit to keep shareholders contented while at the same time pursuing a variety of other objectives such as the growth or the long-term stability of the firm. In such cases costs may *not* be at the minimum level technically feasible for the firm. One possibility is that an organisation's behaviour is determined more by its size than by its ownership. Thus large organisations in both the public sector and the private sector may be 'lazy' in the sense that they do not strive for full technical efficiency.

It is extremely difficult to make judgements on the nature of motivation and on the objectives of people and firms, but we need to be careful that we do not fall into the trap of comparing *actual* public sector corporations with textbook versions of private sector firms which simply assume profit maximisation.

Point (b) is perhaps less controversial. Competition is widely regarded as being a spur to reducing costs and prices and to better meeting consumer wishes. But the fact of private production does not by itself guarantee the existence of competition. This is indicated by the extent to which a small number of firms dominate many industries. One measure of this domination is the five-firm concentration ratio which shows the proportion of output in an industry, or product grouping, accounted for by the five largest firms. Table 3.1 gives five-firm concentration ratios for selected product groups in the UK. In 1977 over half of the industries in the

Table 3.1 Five-firm concentration ratios for selected industries, UK, 1977

Industry	No. of enterprises	% of industry sales of 5 largest firms
Plastics products	683	11.8
General printing and publishing	1,037	14.8
Manufactured stationery	268	31.0
Paint	95	48.8
Soft drinks	123	55.7
Cocoa, chocolate, confectionary	104	67.9
Soaps and detergents	46	82.7
Watches and clocks	16	85.9
Fertilizers	27	91.2
Man-made fibres	9	96.1

Source: Business Monitor, PO/1006

UK had a five-firm concentration ratio of greater than 50 per cent.

Milton Friedman and others put forward an entirely different argument to those considered above in favour of private production. This is simply the value judgement that the most important individual freedom is the *freedom to choose*. The 'freedom to choose' is then defined to mean the absence of government intervention in the economy. This proposition can be neither proved nor disproved. Very little can be said about it other than that people are free to accept it or reject it. Acceptance implies opposition to any government intervention in the economy aimed at reducing inequalities in society.

3.3.2 Contracts and competition

The basic case for contracting-out is that the periodic competition for government contracts forces firms to provide a satisfactory product and to be technically efficient (that is, to keep costs down to the minimum level technically feasible). One problem, however, of contracts as a means by which the private sector can provide commodities to the public sector, is that during the life of a contract the contractor becomes a monopoly supplier and is not subject to the forces of competition which are meant to ensure product quality. Indeed, with the contract price agreed at the outset, profit maximising firms have an incentive to hold costs down, perhaps by keeping the quality of the work as low as possible without attracting government attention.

The government may cancel contracts during the contract period but only if it can demonstrate that the firm is not meeting its contractual obligations. This would require strict criteria to be set and close inspection of the operation of the firm. Even changing the contractor between contracts may involve costs, for instance in the form of lost experience. The inertia of government or its unwillingness to admit a mistake may also limit the extent to which product quality can be maintained in this way.

Hence supporters of public production may claim that the profit motive and competition do not always work to ensure that the public receives the product it wants. This argument takes on greater force if the costs to the community of firms failing to maintain adequate quality are high; or if the costs are only felt many years later. For example, by the time that serious flaws in many council flat tower blocks erected in the 1960s came to light, several of the construction firms were no longer in existence and could not be held responsible for shortcomings in their work.

There is also a need to maintain a strict 'contract relationship' to prevent the contract price of long-term contracts escalating considerably beyond any reasonable allowance for inflation. In particular, there has been great difficulty in keeping under control the costs of many defence projects. Examples include AWAC and the Trident missile system.

In addition, private firms may seek to increase contract profits by hiring workers at lower wage rates and/or with worse work conditions than the government itself could do. Until recently the government felt a particular responsibility towards workers producing commodities which it required. Consequently it sought through the Fair Wages Resolution of the House of Commons (first passed in 1891 and renewed each year) to impose conditions on companies competing for government contracts. Again, of course, inspection by government was required to ensure compliance with these conditions.

However, the repeal of the Fair Wages Resolution in 1983 signalled a change of approach. The government now believes it should use its power as a major purchaser of commodities to cause national real wage levels to fall. Critics of the government suggest that it has encouraged private firms with government contracts to lower the wages and worsen the conditions of service of their employees. This policy, though, may lead to a lower quality labour being hired and/or to a reduction in worker morale, with lower quality work resulting. Further, it is not clear that pushing down the wages of workers who are in many cases among the lowest paid groups in the economy, will have any impact on the wages of other workers.

Finally, a positive case can be made for 'in-house production' (that is, direct public sector production of commodities) based upon the building up over many years of expertise and knowledge of local needs. In-house production may also be argued to be more flexible in cases where contracts are difficult to specify because government requirements are not clear at the outset of a project.

All of this would seem to suggest that we cannot, on theoretical grounds, show that contracting government work out to the private sector necessarily results in a more satisfactory outcome from the point of view of the community than direct public production. There may be budgetary reasons for a government wanting public services to be of lower quality and lower cost and contracting-out may be one way of achieving that. This, however, is quite different from the defence of contracting-out on the grounds that the private sector is more efficient than the public sector.

3.3.3 The mixed provision of social goods

Major debates have gone on in recent years concerning health and education services and housing. One major argument for government provision of a large part of these services is that they are so vital to people's opportunities in life and to their overall welfare that they should be regarded as a *right*, or as a 'badge of citizenship' (that is, something to which every citizen is entitled). A weaker version of this is that everyone should have access to some acceptable level of such important commodities irrespective of their wealth and income. It could be argued that a universal minimum could be achieved through, for instance, an entirely private health or education system with the government subsidising the health insurance or the school fees of the poor. But this does not take into account the rights of citizenship argument. There is a considerable difference in spirit between a scheme which makes payments to some people to allow them to buy services they could not otherwise afford and one which provides a service free to everyone.

A second argument relates to the concept of **externalities**, proposing that it is in the interests of the whole community for everyone to have a certain level of, say, education and medical treatment. External benefits are thought to accrue to the economy, for example, from allowing all children the educational opportunities to use their abilities to the full. This is seen as justifying state education subsidies. Some economists identify a particular form of externality known as **a caring externality**. The idea here is that a community gains from the knowledge that it is looking after those of its members who are in need. It is then argued that such an externality requires the direct provision of the services in question to people in need of them. For this reason it is proposed that the services must be provided universally free of charge. A special application of the argument is made to the health care case. It is claimed that health services should be rationed not by price and the ability to pay (as is the case with market provision) but on the basis of need with equal need being equally treated. This view sees the National Health Service as a 'second best' method (that is, the best practical method) of subsidising the poor and ensuring that those in need receive treatment.

In contrast, a third argument in favour of government intervention provides support only for government financing of health and education services rather than for government production. This is based on the great uncertainties which people face in trying to estimate their future health care needs. This problem may be overcome by government-supported insurance schemes.

Fourthly, lack of knowledge of the costs and benefits of health and education services is often stressed. This leads to the **merit goods** argument that people ought to spend a certain proportion of their incomes on such things as housing, education and health and would do so if they had full knowledge of costs and benefits. Government intervention of one kind or another is then recommended to ensure that this happens. The merit goods approach can be applied also to the question of the type of services to be provided. Thus, it can be proposed that without government intervention resources may be devoted excessively to meeting easily quantifiable goals (such as good exam results) or to satisfying 'popular' needs, such as those for cosmetic surgery or for newsworthy and dramatic operations at the expense of less visible needs like the educational needs of sub-normal children or the health needs of the old and poor.

Friedman, however, points out that government intervention may cause adverse externalities (external costs) in the form of inefficiency, lack of choice, curtailment of freedom and so on. It follows that for government intervention to be justified, the external benefits have to be clearly greater than the associated costs. On this basis it is sometimes argued that government intervention in education should be limited to the achievement of adequate standards in the 'three Rs'.

The whole question of the extent and the type of government intevention desirable in the provision of these services can be seen to involve important areas of social and economic philosophy.

3.3.4 Nationalised industries

The case for nationalisation of certain industries rests on two principal bases:

1. That the industries in question are characterised by such large economies of scale that, given the market size, the industry should, from the point of view of long-run resource allocation, be dominated by a single firm; hence, competition could not be guaranteed to lead to efficiency; *and*
2. That the industries generate large external benefits, making private profit maximisation an undesirable goal from a social viewpoint.

With regard to point (1), however, empirical studies suggest that in most industries, economies of scale are large at low output levels and decline as output increases. Long-run average cost curves often finally become horizontal at a high output level. This has led to the view that typical long-run average cost curves are L-shaped rather than U-shaped as proposed in microeconomic theory. This can be interpreted in two ways. Firms may not have to be particularly large in order to reap most of the benefits available through economies of scale. Equally, very large monopolies may not be subject to significant diseconomies of scale.

Regarding (2), the external benefits may be of a variety of types. We could argue, for example, that industries such as transport, telecommunications and electricity are part of the infrastructure of the economy and that the costs of their products are an important influence on the international competitiveness of British firms. Similarly, we could argue that long-run planning of certain vital areas of the economy is an essential requirement for economic and social policies. Thus, we could stress the need for a comprehensive energy policy and claim that such a policy would be much easier to devise and to carry out if all the principal energy sources were owned and controlled by the government. Or, again, we could emphasise the long time horizon and/or the high risk of investment projects in these areas and suggest that private sector control would place greater weight on the need for short-run profits leading to inadequate investment and short-sighted investment decisions.

Alternatively, we could mention the important impact some industries have on the distribution of income among regions as well as among income classes. Whatever the form of the external benefits, the view being proposed here is that they can be better dealt with by state action than by private markets.

A critic could reasonably contend that nationalisation has not produced a comprehensive energy policy and has not always been associated with sound planning. The objectives of nationalised industries have frequently been changed by governments and it is not clear that investment has often been either adequate or wise. This, however, is not necessarily an argument for privatisation, but rather a criticism of the way in which successive governments have set guidelines for the operation of the nationalised industries. An argument for privatisation must rest mainly on a rejection of our two central points above. Thus, we might feel that privatisation will, via the profit motive, keep costs to the minimum level that is technically feasible and that competition will also keep costs down and ensure the appropriate type and quality of product.

In practice, the privatisation debate has been muddied by a number of other issues which are difficult to assess. Some of these are short-term in nature, such as the desire of the government to raise revenue by selling off the nationalised industries, or by selling off government-held shares in private corporations in order to reduce the public sector borrowing requirement (PSBR). Others are plainly political such as the notion that selling British Telecom shares to large numbers of individuals would be a step towards the development of a 'share-owning democracy'.

Sometimes, too, it is hard to be sure of the grounds on which the arguments are being conducted. For instance, supporters of privatisation seem to suggest that private ownership is necessarily associated with less bureaucracy, more consideration to customers and greater energy and initiative of workers. Yet it is not clear whether these benefits are held to flow from the search for higher profits, from greater competition or from some other indefinable quality of private firms. Here, too, differences of opinion are so much bound up with differences in political and social philosophy that the conflict will never be resolved by appeals to economics alone.

3.4 A consideration of the evidence

There have been a number of attempts to compare the relative performances of public and private sector enterprises. The aim has been to find cases where the differences between a public sector and a private sector enterprise can be seen to relate to the form of ownership rather than to other factors. This has usually meant cases where the two enterprises produce a similar type of output. Some studies have concentrated on measures of productivity, but there have been many difficulties in obtaining the sort of data needed to give adequate measures of productivity. The outcome has been that in studies such as those comparing public and private sector railway companies in Canada or public and private sector airline companies in Australia there is no significant evidence that productivity is lower in public sector than in private sector companies. This conclusion also applies to studies concerning productivity in the public and private sectors in Britain.

One of the better known British studies is that of R. Pryke in 1971. Pryke compared rates of growth of productivity for a number of nationalised industries with the estimated rate of growth of productivity for the manufacturing sector of the economy as a whole. The results of his study are set out in Table 3.2.

Table 3.2 Productivity growth in public and private enterprises

Annual average percentage growth rates of output per unit of composite input 1948–68

Nationalised industries					Private sector manufacturing
Electricity	Coal	Railways	Gas	Airways	
3.4	1.7	1.1	2.2	8.4	2.0

Source: R. Pryke (1971) *Public Enterprise in Practice*, London

Pryke concluded that the performance of the nationalised industries was probably slightly better than that of private manufacturing industry. However, it should be noted that Pryke was comparing only *rates of growth* of productivity, not *levels* of productivity. Thus, nothing could be concluded from the study about the likely effects of privatisation on the productivity of different industries.

American studies on the cost of electric power also fail to support the view that public electricity companies have a lower productivity or higher unit costs than private firms. The principal area in which studies *do* seem to support the private sector is that of refuse collection. Studies in both the United States and Canada have found that franchise and contract arrangements involve lower costs than municipal provision, though there are considerable problems in comparing outputs and in taking proper account of differences in input prices. A recent survey of all the available evidence has considered these various problems and has concluded that: '. . . there is no systematic evidence that public enterprises are less cost effective than private firms' (Millward *et al.* 1983: 258). The authors, however, acknowledge the inadequacy of the available data.

3.5 The management of nationalised industries

The central issue in the running of a nationalised industry is the establishment of its objectives. The next concern is to establish how to assess whether these objectives are being met. The performance of private firms is principally judged on financial grounds, especially the rate of profit earned on capital employed. This is logical since it is assumed that the rate of profit is the main interest of private shareholders and that the central objective of the firm is profit maximisation.

In one sense, the real rate of profit (that is, the rate of profit after allowing for inflation) is also of great importance for the nationalised industries. If we are concerned to allocate capital (a scarce factor of production) wisely in the economy, we will want to ensure that the public sector is using the capital available to it *at least as efficiently* as the private sector is. One way of trying to ensure that this is the case is to judge public sector performance by a private sector criterion – in other words, to establish a real rate of return on capital which is regarded as acceptable in the private sector and then to require capital invested in nationalised industries to earn at least that rate. This was the notion behind both the test discount rate (TDR) introduced in 1967 as a target for individual public enterprise investment projects and its replacement, the real rate of return on assets (R RR). R RR was introduced in the 1978 government White Paper on the nationalised industries. It was initially set at a rate of 5 per cent and was to be applied to investment in the nationalised industries as a whole.

In another way, however, it is the *level* of profit or loss (or of financial surplus or deficit) for the nationalised industries which is of particular interest to the government. A financial deficit will, after all, have to be met by central government through levying higher rates of taxation or through additional government borrowing. A financial surplus, on the other hand, will allow the government to reduce the PSBR or taxation rates or to increase government expenditure elsewhere in the economy.

It is this view which leads to a rather different financial objective for nationalised industries – that they should be required to *break even*, so that they are not imposing a financial burden on the rest of the economy. There are, however, three major difficulties associated with the setting of financial targets for nationalised industries:

1. the question of the relationship between pricing and efficiency;
2. the social role of nationalised industries;
3. the problem of financing investment.

3.5.1 Pricing and efficiency

The first stems from the monopoly position of the nationalised industries. We can see what happens when a monopoly seeks a purely financial target by examining the case of a monopoly seeking to maximise profits. According to microeconomic theory, it will seek to produce at the point at which marginal revenue (MR) is equal to marginal cost (MC). However, because of its monopoly position, the firm's demand curve will slope down and its marginal revenue will be less than the price it charges for its goods; that is, price will be greater than marginal cost.

This conflicts with the basic rule for efficient resource allocation in an economy (derived from the perfect competition case) that price should equal marginal cost. The outcome is the familiar one that monopolies intent on maximising profits will produce *less* output and sell it at a *higher* price than would result from the most efficient allocation of resources.

It is this notion that led to the idea of **marginal cost pricing** –
that since nationalised industries are not constrained by financial
requirements to the same extent as private firms, they should aim
to produce that level of output which achieves maximum social
efficiency, rather than maximum profits. According to an important
theory in welfare economics, known as **Pareto optimality**, a socially
efficient allocation of resources will only be achieved when price
equals marginal cost. At any other price/output solution it will be
possible to reallocate resources so as to make someone better off
without making anyone worse off.

One major problem here is that this policy must produce a
financial *loss* in any industry which experiences long-run declining
costs. This is demonstrated in Fig. 3.1.

In Fig. 3.1 we can see that a nationalised industry acting to
equalise price and marginal cost will produce OA of output and sell
it at a price of OP_1. However, average cost at this level of output
will be OP_2 and the industry will be making a financial loss of P_2P_1
on each unit of output produced and sold. It follows equally that
an industry experiencing increasing costs will make a financial
surplus by following the price equals marginal cost rule, though

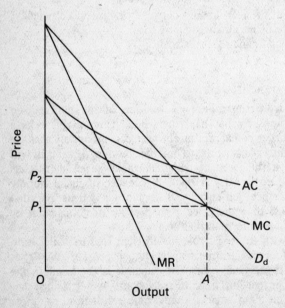

Fig. 3.1 Marginal cost pricing with decreasing costs

the surplus would be less than would be produced by following a marginal revenue equals marginal cost pricing rule.

Consider the decreasing cost case of our diagram where marginal cost pricing would produce a financial deficit. As we said above, this deficit would have to be met by reducing government expenditure elsewhere in the economy, by increasing rates of taxation or by increasing the PSBR. Each of these may lead to inefficiencies elsewhere in the economy. Thus, if taxation does have a strong disincentive effect, raising taxes to finance the financial deficits of nationalised industries may lead, for instance, to a reduction in the amount of work performed in the economy.

How important this issue is *in practice* depends, of course, on whether higher taxes do have strong disincentive effects (an issue which we considered in Chapter 2) or whether a higher PSBR does lead to higher rates of inflation or higher interest rates (an issue we consider in Chapter 6). Clearly, though, the difficulty in principle arises from attempting to apply a rule (price = marginal cost) derived from a model in which perfect competition prevails throughout to a world with manifold market imperfections. In perfect competition, firms operate at minimum average costs and marginal cost pricing produces neither a financial deficit nor a financial surplus.[1]

Indeed, in an economy in which most firms are imperfectly competitive, the action of a few nationalised industries to determine output and price levels *as if* they were in perfect competition may not lead to an improvement in the resource allocation of the economy. It may even make things worse. If all firms are in perfect competition, we can say that resources are being optimally allocated, in the sense of reaching a Pareto optimal solution, when price is set equal to marginal cost. At anything short of this ideal, it is not possible to compare different combinations of perfectly and imperfectly competitive firms. For instance, if a nationalised industry *were* to follow a marginal cost pricing rule, this move towards fulfilling the rules *necessary* for Pareto optimality may *not* in fact lead it nearer to such an allocation. As long as there are imperfections elsewhere (such as externalities, profit maximising monopolists etc.), the marginal cost pricing rule will not, by itself, be *sufficient* to bring about Pareto optimality. This is the basis of an important idea in economics known as the principle of the **second best**. The difficulty is that perfect competition, like innocence, is an absolute. We cannot talk about relative degrees of perfection.

It can be argued, therefore, that a nationalised industry following marginal cost pricing, while private firms are operating at something approximating to $MR = MC$, will be producing relatively too large an output and will be commanding a higher proportion of the economy's resources than is desirable. This proposition naturally leads us back to the idea that nationalised industries should produce financial surpluses which provide rates of return on capital equivalent to those earned in the private sector.

3.5.2 The social role of nationalised industries

A second and quite different objection to the use of financial targets for judging the performance of nationalised industries stems from one of the basic arguments for their existence. This is that nationalised industries generate important external benefits. It follows that it is inappropriate to judge them on the basis of the *private* costs and *private* benefits which enter into market decisions. This view always suggests that the output of nationalised industries should be larger than that indicated by market criteria. We can best explain the argument by looking at a few of the many important public debates in this area.

(a) Employment and balance of payments considerations
We might argue for a large coal industry operating with a considerable financial deficit on the grounds that this is preferable to increased unemployment (and social security payments) and to increased importation of coal. This argument might also be applied to the steel industry.

(b) Environmental damage
We might propose an expanded rail network operating with a financial deficit in preference to the environmental damage wrought by ever-bigger lorries and ever-more miles of motorway. Similarly, we might favour subsidising heavily public transport systems in large cities to avoid private transport clogging the streets and to reduce the number of injuries and deaths on the roads. Or again, we might prefer to subsidise coal production rather than run the unknown risks associated with the use of nuclear power.

(c) Benefits to non-users
We might wish to run late-night and weekend public transport even though it runs at a loss because we might wish to take account of: (i) the benefit to people who almost always catch the 8 p.m. train home of the existence of a 10 p.m. train; or (ii) the benefit

of weekend public transport to people who only use it occasionally but who gain from having the choice available.

(d) Acceptance of risk

We might think it a good idea to subsidise nationalised industries so that they can undertake investment projects which are risky but which may produce technological advances of benefit to the economy as a whole. Or we may allow a nationalised industry to run at a financial loss in order to undertake investment projects which will only produce results well into the future.

(e) Income redistribution

We may use nationalised industries as the means of achieving desired income redistributions. For instance, British Rail may be requested to keep railway fares in country areas below the break-even price level in order to redistribute income towards country dwellers. This may be part of a policy which attempts to dissuade people from moving from the country to the city. Alternatively, a nationalised industry could be asked to keep down prices to the old or to the poor.

You can no doubt provide many examples of arguments in favour of allowing a nationalised industry to run at a financial loss for social reasons. The problems with this approach is that the decisions as to levels of service and sizes of subsidies become entirely political and subject to change for political reasons. Further, under these circumstances it becomes difficult to assess the performance of the nationalised industries. One can attempt to measure labour productivities in the public and private sectors, but as we have pointed out in our summary of evidence above, this is not at all easy to do.

3.5.3 The financing of investment

The third major difficulty associated with the setting of financial targets is that too great a concern with them may lead the government to require nationalised industries to finance all or a lot of their investment from current revenue. Examples of this can be seen in government policy towards the gas and water industries in recent years. This is not, however, how most private sector firms behave – they borrow in order to obtain funds for investment projects. Restricting the ability of nationalised industries to borrow may well lead to under-investment in those industries and to a decline in the quality of the capital stock over time.

3.6 Pricing and profitability in the two sectors

Much has been made of the lack of profitability of nationalised industries in the UK. Certainly, rates of profit of the public corporations have been consistently well below those of the private company sector and in many years, when government subsidies are allowed for, have been negative.

It has also been found in studies of the electricity supply and transport industries in North America that the prices of public firms are less closely related to the marginal costs of producing different commodities than is the case with comparable private firms. The public firms tend in fact to have *lower* prices and *higher* output levels. Whatever the discrepancy in price and output or in profit rates between the public and private sectors we cannot necessarily regard these discrepancies as undesirable. As we have seen above, such outcomes may be justified if they arise from explicit attempts to achieve social goals. If they occur as a result of political influence, for example in an attempt to achieve macro-economic targets, the nationalised industry cannot be held responsible. It is only if it can be clearly demonstrated that the apparently poorer performance of nationalised industries arises from a lack of effort or initiative of the workforce or from bureaucratic management that we can use such figures to support an argument for privatisation.

Notes

1. In this section we have not been making an allowance for normal profits. It would be possible to draw cost curves including as part of costs, a rate of return on capital equal, say, to the average earned in the private sector. Then, following a $P = MC$ rule in the decreasing cost case may produce a financial surplus but would produce a lower rate of return than the private sector average.

Further reading

The arguments supporting the nationalisation of industries can be found in many books. Some recommended sources are the chapter by Peston in Grant and Shaw (1980), Ch. 25 of Morris (1985) and Ch. 8 of Griffiths and Wall (1984). The privatisation debate has spawned a great deal of readily accessible material. Much of this is in the readily available bank reviews, in particular, articles by Shackleton (*National Westminster Bank Quarterly Review*, May 1984), Peacock (*The Three Banks Review*, Dec. 1984), Kay and Silberston (*Midland Bank Review*, Spring 1984) and Beesley and Littlechild (*Lloyds Bank Review*, July 1983). Other useful material can be found in the journals, *Fiscal Studies* and *Political Quarterly*. The February 1984, issue of *Fiscal Studies* contained a recommended article by D. Heald as well as other articles. D. Heald's book, *Public Expenditure* (1983) also deals with the privatisation issue as well as with much else of interest. Griffiths and Wall (1984) provides a brief summary of arguments for and against privatisation.

The best short summary of the arguments for government intervention in health care can be found in Cullis and West (1979). Anyone interested in the argument about 'caring externalities' should consult Culyer (1980). The best summary of arguments about the role of government in education is probably in Ch. 6 of Grant and Shaw (1980). The view of economics which stresses freedom of choice is, of course, developed in M. and R. Friedman (1980).

The evidence regarding the performance of public and private sector enterprises is very well covered in Millward *et al.* (1983). Pryke (1981) provides a very detailed study of the performance of nationalised industries from 1968 on. Pricing policies of nationalised industries and government legislation regarding nationalised industries can be found in sources such as Grant and Shaw (1980) Ch. 3, Maunder (1982) Ch. 3, Morris (1985) and Griffiths and Wall (1984).

Questions

*: Answers to these questions are discussed in Part II below.

1.* To what extent can the efficiency of a nationalised industry be judged from the size of its financial surplus or deficit? (London, June 1983)

2.* Discuss the *economic* arguments for reducing the role of the state in the provision of health, education and housing in the UK. (AEB, June 1985)

3.* Consider some of the reasons for any *one* nationalised industry making persistent financial losses, and discuss whether such losses should be eliminated. (London, June 1984)

4. 'Privatisation represents by far the most effective means of extending market forces and in turn improving efficiency.' Explain what is meant by efficiency in economics and discuss whether or not you agree with this statement about British industry. (JMB, June 1983)

Chapter four
Control of the market economy

The performance of markets is frequently judged by comparing them with the ideal of perfectly competitive markets. These, it is argued, would produce the most efficient allocation of an economy's scarce resources. They would do this because competition would force firms to produce at the minimum point on their average cost curves while producing commodities which would win the approval of consumers. At the same time, perfectly competitve markets would lead to a distribution of income based upon the contributions of workers and entrepreneurs to production. Technically speaking each factor of production (labour, capital etc.) would receive a return equal to its marginal revenue product (that is, equal to the value of the goods and services contributed by the last unit of the factor employed). If all this were true, social welfare would also be at a maximum, in the sense of reaching a Pareto optimal allocation of resources (see Ch. 3).

However, because actual markets are not perfectly competitive it is usually accepted that scope exists for government intervention in markets to increase social welfare. We have considered arguments for government intervention arising from the existence of public goods and of externalities in Chapter 1. Now we turn to the question of the relationship between the **structure** of product markets (that is, the number, size and nature of firms in a market) and the **conduct** and **performance** of firms within those markets. By 'conduct' we mean the policies followed by firms regarding such things as pricing, production and marketing. The 'performance' of a firm refers to the outcome of its conduct in terms of such things as profitability and efficiency.

Here we are interested particularly in the ways in which the structure of markets may differ from the perfectly competitive ideal and in what those differences imply for the behaviour of firms. We can distinguish two principal areas of interest: the number and size of market participants and the extent of integration among firms.

4.1 The number and size of market participants

The starting point is the view that in market economies a strong tendency exists towards monopolisation. Firms *merge* with or *take-over* other firms. As a result markets come to be dominated by a small number of large firms with *market power*. If it can be shown that such developments reduce social welfare (or damage the 'public interest'), there is a case for government intervention to reduce the number of mergers and take-overs. Such action alone may, however, simply lead to firms agreeing formally or informally to act *as if* mergers or take-overs had taken place; that is, firms may remain in separate ownership but may voluntarily restrict competition. Since the outcome from the point of view of the economy as a whole will be the same, any legislation aimed at inhibiting the tendency towards monopolisation will need to be supported by legislation preventing the *restrictive practices* of firms (that is, acts which restrict competition and are thought to be against the public interest).

Naturally, governments will also be interested in likely future developments in markets and will thus be concerned about any restrictions on the ability of new firms to enter markets (*barriers to entry*). Remember, too, that in perfect competition all firms in a market are assumed to be producing exactly the same product. Thus, another feature relevant to the question of how much competition exists in real markets is the extent of *product differentiation*, which may be based on brand names and on advertising, design and packaging as well as on genuine differences between products.

The central point among all this remains, however, whether it is clear that the increase in the market power of firms leads to a reduction in social welfare. This will be influenced not only by the number and size of firms in a market, but by the degree of integration among firms.

4.2 Integration among firms

It is usual to distinguish three types of integration – horizontal, vertical and lateral.

Horizontal integration occurs when firms which are producing the same product combine with each other. Thus, the take-over of Acorn Computers (the manufacturer of the BBC micro computer) by the Italian firm, Olivetti, was an example of horizontal integration.

Vertical integration involves the merging of a firm with one of its suppliers (backward integration) or with a firm which markets or distributes its product (forward integration). An interesting example of backward vertical integration in 1985 was the acquisition by Rupert Murdoch, the television magnate and newspaper publisher, of the famous Hollywood film company, Twentieth Century Fox. Through this take-over, Murdoch obtained access to a film library for his Australian television stations. The brewing industry in Britain provides a good example of forward vertical integration with a high proportion of pubs and off-licences being owned by brewing companies.

Lateral integration involves the merging of firms whose products have nothing in common with each other. A much publicised example of this was the take-over of the retail store group, the House of Fraser Ltd (whose stores include Harrods) by the Al-Fayed brothers, whose other commercial interests were in shipping, oil and the ownership of hotels.

Horizontal integration clearly reduces competition in a particular product market, but so too might vertical and lateral integration. Vertical integration may make it more difficult for new firms to enter the market and compete because they may face problems in obtaining supplies at competitive prices or in distributing and marketing their final products. Lateral integration opens up the possibility that a firm with interests in several markets may be able to operate in one market at a loss in order to prevent a new firm entering that market. That is, they may be able to *cross-subsidise* so as to keep their prices low in those markets in which they would otherwise be vulnerable to new entrants. Governments which are interested in maintaining a certain level of competition in an economy may, then, be concerned not only with the extent to which a proposed merger will lead to the dominance of one particular market by one or a few large firms, but also with the resulting pattern of activities across several markets. However, that still leaves open the question of whether a reduced level of competition in a market economy really is against the public interest.

4.3 Market power and social welfare

The simple case against the monopolisation of markets derives from the notion that a monopoly faces a downward sloping demand curve (average revenue curve) and therefore will always be in a position where its marginal revenue is less than its average revenue. This notion leads on (see sect. 4.3.1 below) to the prediction of a lower output and higher price for a monopoly than for a perfectly competitive firm. However, we shall see that this prediction depends upon the assumption that the average costs of an industry do not vary with the size of firms in that industry. This assumption has to be questioned and other factors have to be taken into account before we can try to make a judgement about the impact on social welfare of reduced competition.

4.3.1 The simple case against monopolies

In Fig. 4.1 we can see what happens to social welfare when a perfectly competitive industry is monopolised.

In this diagram it is assumed that unit costs are constant and hence that average total cost is equal to marginal cost. This assumption is made only to allow the diagram to be followed easily.

In a perfectly competitive industry, all firms will be maximising profits and will be producing at the point where marginal revenue (MR) equals marginal cost (MC). But, since the average revenue curve and the marginal revenue curve are identical in perfect competition, this means they will be producing where price is equal

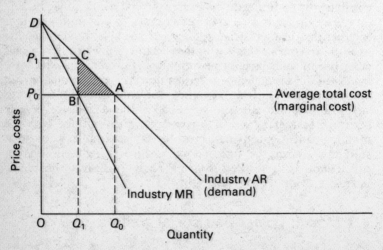

Fig. 4.1 Loss of surplus through monopolisation

to marginal cost. Since this is true for each perfectly competitive firm, it will be true for the industry as a whole. Thus, in Fig. 4.1, the output and the price for the perfectly competitive industry are given at point A, where the MC curve cuts the demand curve. The output is Q_0 and the price is P_0. If we assume that the private costs to the producing firms accurately reflect the costs to society of using scarce resources to produce this output (that is, that there are no social costs), total costs are given by the area P_0AQ_0O. However, the benefits to society (as measured by the total amount people are willing to pay for output Q_0), assuming no social benefits, are given by the area DAQ_0O. There is thus a surplus which accrues to consumers (*consumer surplus*) which arises because a number of consumers would have been willing to pay a higher price for the product than the market price. The consumer surplus, then, is the area DAP_0. There is no surplus accruing to producers in the perfect competition case because all firms will just be earning normal profits.

Consider what happens when the industry is taken over by a single firm. The monopoly's demand curve is *not* a horizontal line since it is identical with the downward-sloping industry demand curve. As a consequence, marginal revenue will be less than average revenue at all output levels. If the monopoly is profit maximising, it will be producing at point B where MR = MC. That is, it will be producing an output of Q_1 and will be able to sell that output at a price of P_1: in this way fulfilling the 'classical' criticism against monopoly of a lower output and a higher price than under perfect competition. Also the consumer surplus is now given by the area DCP_1. In other words, it is smaller than in the perfectly competitive case by the area P_1CAP_0.

However, the firm is making super-normal profits of (AR–AC) × Output. This is shown by the area P_1CBP_0. Two things have happened.

Firstly, there has been a redistribution of income from consumers to producers since the monopoly firm is now receiving a higher price for its product than the price at which it would have been willing to supply the output Q_1. We can say, then, that the higher price disadvantages *consumers* but leads to a gain to producers (that is, it converts some of the consumer surplus into producer surplus).

Secondly, total welfare has fallen. If we compare the two cases, we see that consumer surplus has fallen by *more* than the super-normal profits now being received by the monopoly. This extra amount can be seen to be the shaded area CAB. The community as a whole is worse off in welfare terms because

63

monopolisation has led to an output level for the industry which is smaller than in the perfectly competitive case.

4.3.2 Economies of scale

As we pointed out, however, this case is constructed on the assumption of unchanged average costs. If we assume instead that the single large firm in the monopoly case can take advantage of **economies of scale** (and for many industries this seems to be a reasonable assumption), then it is possible to reverse the argument and show that monopolisation might lead to gains in social welfare. This can be seen in Fig. 4.2.

Here we continue to assume that marginal cost is equal to average total cost, but now we have assumed a much lower level of average total cost (and marginal cost) for the monopoly than for the perfectly competitive industry, because we are assuming that the monopoly is able to take advantage of considerable economies of scale. As a result, even though the monopoly will produce at point B where MR = MC and MR will be less than price, it will produce a higher level of output and sell it at a lower price than would have occurred under perfect competition. In welfare terms we can now see that monopolisation leads to an *increase* indicated by the shaded triangle ACF. Monopolisation could thus in this case be argued to be in the public interest.

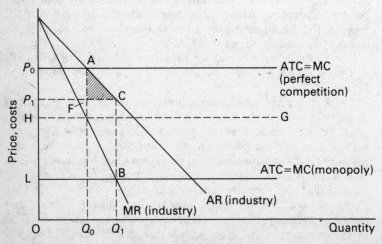

Fig. 4.2 Gain in surplus through economies of scale

In an actual case, it is clear that we would need to know two things: firstly, whether economies of scale would be available to larger firms; and secondly, how great those economies would be likely to be. Examination of Fig. 4.2 shows that for the case for the monopoly to be made, average costs would have to fall below the line *HG*.

4.3.3 Monopolies and x-inefficiency

At this point we need to consider an implicit assumption of the above argument – that the monopoly firm would in practice take full advantage of the cost reductions available due to economies of scale. In other words, it is assumed above that the monopoly produces at minimum cost, even though there is no competitive pressure on it to do so. A little thought about the nature of large organisations suggests that this is an unlikely assumption. It seems reasonable, on the contrary, to assume that some of the gains available to the firm because of lack of competition will be taken not in the form of higher profits but in the form of greater ease for both management and workers. Consider the case illustrated in Fig. 4.2 once more. Our monopoly may technically be able to produce an output of Q_1 at an average total cost of OL but may behave in such a way that its *actual* average cost curve lies above LB (perhaps along HG). Then, even if it is following profit maximising price rules, it will produce a lower output and charge a higher price than is indicated for a monopoly in the diagram. It is this notion of scarce resources being in a sense wasted that is known as x-inefficiency.

What we have, then, are two quite separate ideas of inefficiency. The first is that because of the structure of the industry in the perfect competition case firms may be too small to be able to take advantage of potential economies of scale. Each firm may be acting in a **technically efficient** manner, in that each is producing at the minimum point of its average cost curve. However, the industry as a whole is economically inefficient since its total output could be produced at a lower cost in terms of resources.

The second is that although changing the structure of the industry to a monopoly may provide opportunities for cutting costs, these may not in fact be realised because lack of competition may lead the monopoly to produce above its minimum cost level. That is, the monopoly may act inefficiently in a technical sense. What this means is that we need more than merely *technical* information about the extent to which economies of scale become available as firms become larger. To compare properly perfect competition with monopoly we must know *how* large firms behave as the degree of competition is reduced.

4.3.4 The size of firms and the level of research

The need to know how firms behave in practice is increased when we allow for the possibility of technological change. If we assume that technological change leads to an increase in the total output obtainable from our scarce resources, we need to look at factors which will encourage technological change. One obvious possibility is that large firms earning super-normal profits have much greater scope for undertaking the research necessary for technological progress. In the usual jargon of economists, we can say that even if a monopoly performs poorly in terms of **static efficiency** (that is, assuming no technological change), its existence may be justified on *dynamic* grounds. We need to know, however, whether the possible links between firm size and technological progress do, in fact, exist.

4.3.5 Monopolies and the inadequacy of theory

What does seem clear is that we cannot judge the impact on the public interest of reduced competition in markets from economic theory alone. Equally, the outcome may be different in different cases. An increase in market power may be associated with a reduction in costs through economies of scale and with increased research expenditure and more rapid technological change. On the other hand, it may lead to x-inefficiency and the failure to make full use of scarce resources. A government must decide, then, whether every single case has to be decided on its individual merits or whether certain types of market structure are sufficiently likely to be against the public interest that they should be ruled out automatically.

4.4 The evidence

When we talk, then, of the likely impact of changes in the structure of markets on the *performance* of firms, we are talking specifically about the outcome in terms of profitability, efficiency and technical progress.

There is little evidence that the first two of these elements of performance, profitability and efficiency, are significantly improved as a result of the growth of firms through mergers. The most profitable firms are not necessarily large. In addition, the majority of firms which take over other firms seem to be growth maximisers rather than profit maximisers. The desire for growth may be fuelled by managerial ambitions for higher pay, or greater esteem or power. Alternatively, a firm may seek to grow to reduce the risk that it will be taken over at a later date. Again, firms may merge to allow an orderly reduction of capacity in an industry facing falling demand or in an attempt to resist foreign competition. There has been a wide variety of UK studies of merger activity. For example, in 1970 Newbold published the results of a study of thirty-eight mergers which had taken place between 1967 and 1968 which showed that in only 18 per cent of cases did firms admit to being motivated by any possible gains from economies of scale. Much more important seemed to be the attempt to reduce risk and control markets. Cowling, Cubbin and Hall in a 1980 study of nine major mergers also stressed the generation of greater market power through mergers and concluded that resulting economies of scale were difficult to identify. Whittington, also in 1980, found that the level of profitability is unrelated to firm size. Other studies (for instance by Singh in 1971 and Meeks in 1977) have shown that many mergers actually lead to a fall in the combined profitability of the merging firms.

In summary, we can say that few mergers seem to be made in order to reap the benefits of technical economies of scale. Indeed, many mergers do not result in larger plant sizes. The growing firm may simply acquire more plants. There may be economies of scale in management or in the rationalisation of plant activities within the now larger firm but it is not at all certain that mergers lead to greater efficiency. Further, there appears to be considerable evidence that scope exists for reducing costs significantly within many large firms with a great deal of market power.

Finally, the link between size and technical innovation seems to be very insecure. In many industries it is the smaller, sometimes newer, firms which lead the way here. Larger firms in some cases lack the necessary flexibility or have too much of their capital tied up in existing technologies. Large firms which do invest heavily in research may establish a lead in the *invention* of new products and processes. It does not necessarily follow, however, that they will choose to put these inventions into practice (that is, invention may not be followed by *innovation*).

In sum, the practical case in favour of movements away from

67

competition is not strong. But this does not mean that movements towards greater competition are always desirable. It must be borne in mind that such movements may involve redistributions of income and that where these occur it may be impossible to decide whether the country as a whole is better off as a result of the change.

4.4.1 The removal of cross-subsidisation

Interesting examples of this arise where limited competition has been associated with the growth of cross-subsidisation among the firm's customers. One particular example is the national bus industry. Here, limited competition over the years has allowed firms to use part of the profits from peak hour and city routes to continue to provide unprofitable services at unpopular hours or to thinly populated country areas. Increased competition may then simply mean increased competition on profitable routes. The loss of profits on these routes by the companies who had previously faced only limited competition may lead to a reduction in the number of unprofitable services. Clearly there would be a redistribution of income and it would be difficult to say whether people as a whole were better off. Indeed, once externalities are allowed for, it may well be that in such cases greater competition is against the public interest. Similar arguments have been put forward in recent years in relation to the deregulation of the services provided by opticians and to proposals to introduce greater competition into the telecommunication industry, the health services industry and many others.

4.5 What should be controlled?

These arguments seem to reinforce the view that individual cases should be investigated, rather than having blanket legislation which assumes that increased competition is necessarily 'good' and that the reduction of competition beyond some particular point is necessarily 'bad'. One problem, however, is that the investigation of individual cases takes considerable time and uses resources. In addition, it raises difficulties over the basis of choice of the cases to be investigated and introduces the possibility of political influence on this choice or on the subsequent investigations.

4.5.1 The British approach

British legislation has accepted the selective approach to the judgement of the impact on competition of mergers and of restrictive practices. The major British legislation in this field is considered below.

The first British legislation was the Monopolies and Restrictive Practices (Inquiry and Control) Act of 1948. This set up the Monopolies Commission which was given the duty of inquiring into the behaviour of monopolies referred to it by a government department known as the Board of Trade. A monopoly position in a market was defined as one where a firm (or group of firms acting together) controlled at least one-third of the supplying, processing or producing of goods and used this degree of control to restrict competition. The criteria to be used to investigate the conduct of firms referred to the Commission reflected fully the perfect competition ideal and the possible departures from it which we have considered here. Thus, the Commission was to be concerned with **allocative efficiency** (the allocation of scarce resources so that the commodities desired by consumers could be produced at the lowest possible cost); with **x-efficiency** or **productive efficiency** (the requirement that firms take advantage of potential economies of scale and do in practice keep costs to a minimum) and **dynamic efficiency** (the full encouragement of technical change and the full development of markets).

Apart from the fact that the Act was limited by not being applied to service industries, nationalised industries or trade unions, the principal problems were not with the ideas behind the legislation but with the way it was put into operation. Firstly, the Monopolies Commission was small – being limited to a maximum of ten members – and this contributed to the slowness of the investigations undertaken (often longer than two years). Secondly, the government was more concerned with the effects of restrictive practices than with the presence of monopolies, and most references to the Commission between 1949 and 1956 dealt with restrictive practices. Indeed, in this period only two inquiries were made into industries dominated by large firms. Thirdly, many of the recommendations of the Commission were not put into practice by the government.

In 1953 the permissible size of the Commission was increased to twenty-five and the use of sub-groups of members was allowed, to attempt to speed up investigations. In 1956 the Restrictive Trade Practices Act removed from the Monopolies Commission the task of investigating restrictive practices by setting up the separate Restrictive Practices Court. This allowed the Commission to concentrate on monopoly markets, but still few references were made to it. Investigations into only four industries were completed between 1956 and 1965. Governments remained more interested in restrictive practices than in market concentration.

In 1965, however, the Monopolies and Mergers Act was passed. This extended the powers of the Commission in two significant ways. Firstly, it provided for references to it to enable it to investigate *proposed* mergers which would produce a monopoly structure in an industry. From 1973 the definition of such a structure was tightened to allow references of proposed mergers which would give a firm a 25 per cent market share. From 1973 also the Commission became known as the Monopolies and Mergers Commission. Secondly, the powers of the Commission were widened to include service industries.

These changes led to an increase in the activity of the Commission, but the position remained that fewer than 3 per cent of mergers eligible for referral to the Commission were in fact referred to it. It is true, however, that referral or fear of referral may be sufficient to block a proposed merger. Of those mergers investigated, about one-third have been found to be against the public interest.

The government can intervene in the investigation process at several points. The decision to refer mergers to the Commission is now taken by the Director General of Fair Trading, a position established in the 1973 Fair Trading Act. The Secretary of State for Industry can, however, overrule the Director General's decision to refer or can decide to make references against the advice of the Director General. Once the Monopolies and Mergers Commission has met and examined a merger, their acceptance or their rejection of the merger can be overruled by the Secretary of State. It is hardly surprising that under these circumstances there has been a great deal of confusion and controversy concerning the operation of the legislation over the years.

In 1980 the Competition Act was passed by Parliament, giving the Director General of Fair Trading new powers to examine anti-competitive practices of individual firms. However, there was no explicit indication of the sort of practices the government had in mind. The Act also allowed the investigation of nationalised industries and of trade unions. The 1980 legislation provides stronger support for the textbook competitive ideal and gives the government considerable potential power over the activities of individual firms. But uncertainty and controversy have remained. In practice, the government has been particularly concerned with the activities of nationalised industries and with the question of competition in the labour market. No coherent or strong policy has emerged towards the growth of corporate power in the private sector of the economy. Even where government corporation or government-held shares in private corporations have been sold off to the private sector, there has been little or no attempt to ensure an increase in the level of competition.

4.5.2 Formal measures of concentration

An alternative approach is the much more rigid policy which is followed in the United States. There a formal measure of market concentration is used as a basis for automatic rejection of proposed mergers where the measure suggests that a high degree of concentration will result, or as a signal to the Justice Department that investigation is required. This has the advantage of being more open and apparently less subject to political manipulation. Firms can calculate in advance whether merger proposals are likely to be accepted or rejected. However, the interpretation of the index used to provide a measure of concentration is still arbitrary. Worse, the index only applies to horizontal mergers. This leads to firms being more likely to merge vertically or laterally. The form of the legislation changes the behaviour of firms, but it is far from clear that it leads to the maintenance of a greater degree of competition overall.

4.6 Other examples of government intervention in industry

4.6.1 The labour market

Over most of this century the view has prevailed that legislation has been necessary to protect workers in a variety of ways. The view that the unorganised worker is at a considerable disadvantage in bargaining with his employer can be traced back at least as far as Adam Smith in *The Wealth of Nations*, published in 1776. A number of pieces of legislation have sought to reduce this disadvantage by providing legal protection for trade unions. Thus the Trade Disputes Act of 1906 gave unions protection from being sued by firms because of losses to firms arising from industrial action. In 1891 the first Fair Wages Resolution of the House of

Commons was passed and in 1909 the Trade Boards Act provided for the fixing of minimum wages in very low-wage industries. Wages councils in their modern form were established by the Wages Council Act of 1945. In 1911, the first unemployment insurance scheme was set up and in 1965 the Redundancy Payments Act was passed. Legislation in the 1970s provided increased employment protection, made it easier for trade unions to form closed shops at workplaces, and under the Health and Safety at Work Act of 1974 extended government powers to control working environments in the interests of workers. 1970 saw the passing into law of the Equal Pay Act. The Employment Protection Act of 1975 placed employers under a legal obligation to disclose information for collective bargaining to recognised trade unions. Various government schemes over the years have provided for job subsidies, the retraining of workers and the enforcement of contributions by firms to industrial training. And so the list could go on.

But in recent years many attitudes behind such legislation have changed. In particular, the switch by governments from the belief that unemployment was largely caused by inadequate demand to the view that the major problem was with the supply side of the economy (a switch discussed in Ch. 7), has led to the idea that government intervention in the labour market should be much reduced.

The Government has put much stress on the notion that the principal cause of unemployment in Britain is high labour costs. This is a controversial view and there is so far little evidence to support it, but it has had a considerable impact on government policy. Since labour costs can be broken down into the wage paid to the worker plus the additional costs of employing workers faced by employers, attempts to alter the nature of the labour market have been aimed at both of these components.

For example, the Government argued that trade unions' bargaining power had become too great. This led to legislation to restrict picketing, to make it more difficult to operate closed shops, to allow trade unions to be sued over the actions of their members during industrial action unless that action has been supported by a majority in a secret ballot. Secret ballots are now also required for elections to the governing bodies of trade unions. This has all been associated with a general view that the 'right of management to manage' should be re-asserted in British industry.

The Government has sought in a variety of ways to lower wage demands and, in particular, has sought to lower the relative wages of the young and the low-paid. In this regard, it has acted to reduce the scope of wages councils, to tie job subsidies to employers of young workers (under the 1982 Young Workers Scheme) to low-paid jobs, to reduce the national insurance contributions of the low-paid and of their employers and so on. Within the public sector, the wage-setting system which operated through comparisons between public and private sector wages has been scrapped.

The attack on non-wage employment costs has also had a number of elements. For example, in designated enterprise zones firms are not subject to many of the legal requirements embodied in health and safety at work and employment protection legislation. The size of inspectorates which have the task of enforcing government legislation dealing with the protection of wages and conditions of work has been reduced and the Government has shown itself generally in favour of reducing employee protection. It has been claimed that other legislation (for instance on pensions, on council house sales, on stamp duty payable on house purchase) will have an impact on the labour market, acting to increase labour mobility and, through this, perhaps keeping wage settlements down. In other words, we have returned once more to the view that markets left to themselves will operate efficiently.

The problems involved in assessing the impact of all of these changes are twofold. Firstly, it is far from clear what, if any, increase in labour demand will follow. Secondly, it is certain that many of the changes will lead to a redistribution of income, possibly away from the poor. As always, it will be very difficult to weigh up the benefits to the gainers and the costs to the losers. Any improvement in the *efficiency* of labour markets may be at the expense of *equity* in the community.

4.6.2 Other markets

Government controls have also been abolished in other markets. Thus, in the capital market we have seen the abolition of controls on foreign exchange transactions (1979), on dividend policies (1979), on bank lending (1980) and on hire-purchase credit (1982). Planning controls have been reduced, firms are required to provide less information to the Registrar of Companies, regional and industrial development policies have been changed. Many other changes have already occurred or are planned. In all of these areas it is difficult to predict the impact on output, employment and income distribution. All that can be said at this stage is that many far-reaching changes have been made to the relationships between government, employees, employers and consumers.

Further reading

The best single source of material on the structure, conduct, performance model of firms is Pappas, Brigham and Shipley (1983). This is also very good in its treatment of government legislation and of the activities of the Monopolies and Mergers Commission. Chapter 5 of Griffiths and Wall (1984) provides a very useful discussion of the various explanations of merger activity (including a summary of empirical evidence) and of attempts to control merger activity. Much more detail is to be found in books by Cowling *et al.* (1980), Prais (1976) and Kuehn (1975). Morris (1985) has a good account of the various aspects of competition policy. Chapter 12 of Hare and Kirby (1984) contains an interesting treatment of the choice between the use of an absolute rule to determine the impact of a merger on the public interest and the case by case approach. This chapter also provides a summary account of UK competition policy in practice. Prest and Coppock (1984) is very useful in this area and also contains a good chapter on the labour market. Legislation affecting the labour market in Britain is comprehensively treated in Bain (1983). Government intentions to reform the labour, capital and goods markets are outlined in the *Economic Progress Report* of Nov./Dec. 1984. The view that government legislation imposes particular burdens on small business is developed in the government report, *Burdens on Business*, published on 31 March 1985. The February 1985 issue of the journal *Fiscal Studies* contained a series of papers on various aspects of competition policy as part of a symposium on the subject.

Questions

*: Answers to these questions are discussed in Part II below.

1.* Why and how may a government attempt to control the growth of private enterprise monopoly power? (ICMA, Nov. 1983)

2.* What criteria might be applied when assessing whether a merger between two firms was in the public interest? (London, June 1983)

3. Outline the broad principles which underlie the legislation on monopoly and restrictive trade practices in Britain. Is an

increase in the degree of competition likely to be of benefit to the economy? (JMB, June 1982)

4. Consider the possible consequences of transforming a monopoly into a perfectly competitive industry. (WJEC, June 1980)

Chapter five
The government sector and stabilisation

5.1 Introduction

In 1985/6, total public spending is expected to be about £140 bn or 41 per cent of total spending in the economy. Even if we remove those expenditures, on social security, which are strictly speaking only a transfer of spending power between private sector members of the economy, the demand which the public sector makes upon goods and services produced in the UK amounts to some 29 per cent.

Plainly, government spending is a large part of total spending in the economy and this means that changes in spending have great potential ability to 'stabilise' (or for that matter to destabilise) the whole economy. This is easily shown by some figures. Take two hypothetical economies. In the first, public spending amounts to 50 per cent of the total. A decision to increase public expenditure by 5 per cent has a 2.5 per cent effect upon the total (50 per cent × 5 per cent). By contrast, in an economy where public spending is, say, only 20 per cent of the total, the same proportionate increase has only a one per cent effect upon total spending (20 per cent × 5 per cent). The inescapable conclusion is that a given percentage change in public spending will have a more significant effect upon total spending when the public sector is large than when it is small; and the same argument can be repeated for changes in taxation and therefore public revenue.

Economists who take a 'Keynesian' view of the economy believe there are sound theoretical reasons for using changes in government spending and revenue to influence the total level of spending in the economy, and that changes in spending cause changes in real output and employment (rather than just the level of prices). Changes in spending and revenue for this purpose are known as 'fiscal policy' and may be regarded as part of the total array of instruments which governments may use for 'demand management' or 'stabilisation'. Given that such changes are, as we established above, more significant with a large public sector, we have some appreciation of why it is that Keynesian economists are more tolerant of (or less critical of) a large public sector than are monetarists, and why there is a greater sympathy for Keynesian economic analysis amongst politicians of the centre and the left than there is amongst those of the right who favour the promotion of free market forces.

5.2 The Keynesian view

We begin by defining an equilibrium level of income as that level of income at which the total of people's planned expenditure is equal to what firms plan to produce. If we refer to 'the total of people's planned expenditure' as aggregate demand (AD), and identify the various categories of spending which make up the total, then we have the expression:

$$AD = C + I + G + X - Z$$

In this expression, C, I, G, and X stand for the spending decisions of, respectively: households (consumption); firms (investment); the government (on consumption and investment goods for the public sector); and foreign buyers (for UK exports). Unfortunately, if we simply aggregate these expenditures as they stand, we shall be including as part of the aggregate demand for UK goods and services some demand (particularly under the consumption heading) which is really a demand for the output of foreign firms. This we correct by deducting the demand for imports, Z, from the total of spending decisions. If we now define equilibrium income as that level of income (or output) which people in the aggregate wish to purchase, we can say that, in equilibrium:

$$Y = C + I + G + X - Z$$

Keynesian economists have three reasons for being very interested in the equilibrium level of income and in the conditions which give rise to it.

5.2.1 Real income

Firstly, we have always to remember that the income, Y, to which we refer is a flow of output of real goods and services. Because it has to be measured and expressed in money terms, and because for most of us our individual incomes take the form of money, the real nature of Y can be overlooked. In fact an increase in Y means that more goods and services are being produced and can therefore be consumed. If we take either of the views that 'more is always better than less' or that 'the fundamental problem in economics is scarcity', there is an obvious welfare gain from maximising the level of income. A high level of income simply means that there is more to go round than would be the case with a low level of income.

5.2.2 Output and employment

A second reason for interest in the equilibrium level of income is that output is related to employment (see Fig. 5.1 below). Other things being equal, we would expect a high level of output to be associated with a high level of employment. The relationship may not be a simple one: changes in output may be accompanied by changes in either productivity or overtime working rather than by changes in the number of people employed. It is also sometimes argued that Keynesian economists have oversimplified the output:employment relationship by ignoring conditions affecting the supply of labour; we shall look at this in more detail in Chapter 7. None the less, Keynesian economists have a valid point in asserting that, beyond narrow limits, output cannot change without an associated change in employment.

5.2.3 Instability

Lastly, it would not of course matter very much that 'income' represents the quantity of real goods and services available to the community nor that it is related to the level of employment, if the level of income tended automatically to assume its maximum possible level. In such circumstances, all would always be for the best and no possible government intervention could improve matters. The belief that the economy does indeed tend normally to this happy situation has in recent times emerged as another criticism of Keynesian economics and again we shall examine this in Chapter 7. The conviction of Keynesians that income does *not* tend automatically to its maximum possible level is based upon a number of detailed arguments which can be briefly summarised under the heading of 'instability'.

It is asserted that some elements at least of aggregate demand are liable to sudden change and that, in consequence, the economy may be in a constant state of change. It may be moving into recession, with falling demand and rising unemployment; or into boom, with rising output and falling unemployment, if there previously was spare capacity; or with static output with rising prices if capacity was already fully utilised. In other words, although the economy might always tend towards an equilibrium position, and indeed might sometimes even arrive at it, the *process* could be lengthy and characterised by many random shocks. Still more importantly, the resulting equilibrium position could occur *at any level* of output and employment.

The source of instability most frequently cited by Keynesian economists has always been private sector investment and some justification for this can be seen from Table 5.1. The standard deviation of a set of figures measures the range of dispersion of those figures each side of their average value. Comparing the standard deviations in Table 5.1, one can see that fluctuations in investment expenditure have been greater than the fluctuations in any other component of expenditure.

This is because the investment decision involves judging a future (and therefore strictly speaking unknown) stream of net earnings against the present cost of the capital equipment. In theory, the wise businessman will:

(a) Estimate the future stream of gross earnings likely to be produced by the capital equipment under consideration;
(b) Deduct from these expected gross earnings the estimated running costs of the equipment;
(c) Apply to these net earnings that rate of discount (the marginal efficiency of capital) which makes their net present value just equal to the cost or 'supply price' of the capital equipment;
(d) Compare that rate of discount with the current rate of interest.

If the rate of discount applied in (c) is equal to or greater than the rate of interest in (d) the project will go ahead. If it is less, the project is not profitable. Clearly, there are a lot of unknowns and a lot of uncertainties in this process:

1. The *future stream of earnings* obviously depends upon the level of sales and the price at which the sales take place. Future earnings could be affected by the behaviour of competitors, who might, for example, introduce a superior product, or it could be affected by changes in consumer tastes. The value of future sales revenue is also likely to depend upon the 'general

Table 5.1 Growth of the components of total final expenditure (TFE) at 1980 prices, 1962–83

(Units: £ bn and percentage change on previous year)

	TFE		Consumption	
	£ bn	%	£ bn	%
1962	176.8	—	91.6	—
1963	184.4	4.3	95.8	4.6
1964	195.5	6.0	98.8	3.1
1965	196.7	0.6	100.4	1.6
1966	203.7	3.6	102.2	1.8
1967	210.7	3.4	104.7	2.4
1968	220.6	4.7	107.8	3.0
1969	224.2	1.6	108.4	0.6
1970	230.4	2.8	111.2	2.6
1971	237.5	3.0	114.7	3.1
1972	246.1	3.6	121.5	5.9
1973	266.7	8.4	127.7	5.1
1974	265.5	−0.4	125.6	−1.6
1975	259.5	−2.3	124.8	−0.6
1976	264.4	1.7	125.1	0.2
1977	272.7	3.1	124.6	−0.4
1978	282.5	3.7	131.5	5.5
1979	292.8	3.6	137.9	4.9
1980	284.6	−2.8	136.9	−0.7
1981	280.2	−1.5	137.0	0.1
1982	287.2	2.7	138.9	1.4
1983	300.4	4.6	144.0	3.7
Average		2.59		2.20
Standard deviation		2.64		2.19

Source: The UK National Accounts, HMSO 1984, Table 2.1

state of the economy'. If it is expanding, sales will generally tend to increase; in recession, they will fall. Once we recognise this, we realise how it is that such diverse influences as wars in the middle east (affecting the price of oil and therefore the real incomes of both oil-producing and oil-importing countries) and the results of general elections (which may shift the

Government consumption		Investment		Exports	
£ bn	%	£ bn	%	£ bn	%
33.1	—	26.4	—	26.1	—
33.7	1.8	27.6	4.5	27.4	5.0
34.3	1.8	34.6	25.4	28.4	3.6
35.2	2.6	34.9	1.0	29.8	4.9
36.1	2.6	34.8	−0.0	31.2	4.7
38.1	5.5	37.4	7.5	31.4	0.6
38.3	0.5	40.0	7.0	35.4	12.7
37.6	−0.2	40.0	—	38.9	9.9
38.1	1.3	40.7	1.8	41.0	5.4
39.3	3.1	40.1	−1.5	43.8	6.8
40.9	4.0	39.5	−1.5	44.3	1.1
42.8	4.6	46.8	18.5	49.5	11.7
43.5	1.6	43.5	−7.0	53.1	7.3
45.8	5.3	37.4	−14.0	51.7	−2.6
46.2	0.9	42.0	12.3	56.3	8.9
45.7	−1.0	42.5	1.2	59.9	6.4
46.7	2.2	43.3	1.9	61.0	1.8
47.6	1.9	44.1	1.8	63.3	3.8
48.4	1.7	36.1	−18.1	63.2	—
48.3	—	32.9	−8.9	61.9	−2.0
49.0	1.4	36.6	11.2	62.8	1.5
50.5	2.9	42.5	16.1	63.3	0.8
	1.89		2.82		4.39
	1.69		10.12		4.12

balance of economic policy between counter-inflation and higher employment) can become relevant.

2. Estimates of *future running costs* are also subject to uncertainty. The politics of the middle east and the future prospects for oil prices again provide an example, and are particularly relevant to investment projects with high energy inputs. Future move-

ments in real wages, in relation to other factor prices, will affect labour-intensive projects. More specifically, individual projects will look more or less attractive depending upon how entrepreneurs *think* wage costs in their industry will move in relation to costs in other industries.

3. Lastly, but most important to any discussion of the public sector and stabilisation, we have to recognise that frequent changes in taxation policy themselves create uncertainty. Depending upon the precise nature of the changes one can show that they can enter the decision-making process at (b), (c) or (d) above. An increase in corporation tax, for example, reduces the proportion of *expected earnings* which a firm can retain for its own use; by contrast, an increase in depreciation allowances has the effect of lowering the *real supply price* of capital equipment; changes in the tax treatment of interest charges change the *effective rate of interest* against which the discounted earnings must be judged.

Given these uncertainties, therefore, it is not surprising that at any given rate of interest the volume of investment expenditure in an economy is likely to fluctuate in line with business 'expectations' or what Keynes more memorably called 'the animal spirits of entrepreneurs'.

In brief then, we may summarise the Keynesian view as being that employment is related to aggregate income (and output), and that this depends upon the level of aggregate demand. However, demand is unstable and therefore governments should be prepared to intervene; both to smooth out the instability of demand and to keep the level of aggregate demand, output and employment at the highest practicable level. We need now to see how it can be done.

5.3 Changes in government spending

One obvious method of influencing aggregate demand is for the government to vary its own expenditure. Figure 5.1 shows a situation where total planned expenditure $(C + I + G + X - Z)$ is equal to current income/output, Y. Thus, Y is an equilibrium level of income.

We shall assume now that at Y there are unused resources and that the economy could expand to Y_f before encountering full employment. The required policy is well known. Total expenditure is increased initially by raising the level of government expenditure,

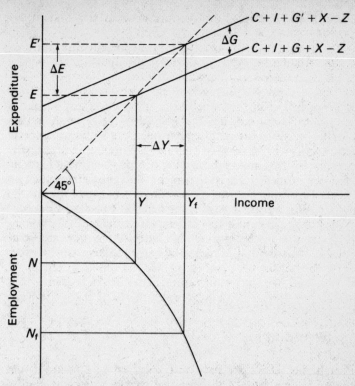

Fig. 5.1 Expenditure and employment

(tax rates unchanged) by an amount, ΔG, which has the effect of shifting vertically the whole expenditure function. Notice, however, that the vertical displacement $(= \Delta G)$ is much smaller than the eventual increase in income (from Y to Y_f). Since equilibrium income is that level of income at which all output is willingly purchased, it follows that total expenditure must also have increased by more than ΔG (from E to E' in fact). In effect, Y (and E) have increased by some *multiple* of the initial change in G: a result of the well known multiplier process. Diagrammatically, we can see that this is a consequence of the expenditure function having a positive slope. If, by contrast, it were horizontal, the vertical displacement, ΔG, would be exactly equal to the ultimate change in Y and E. An interesting exercise is to take Fig. 5.1 and re-draw the expenditure function with a steeper slope and then to displace it by the same vertical distance. It will cut the 45-degree line at a *higher* level of Y, suggesting an even larger multiplier effect.

In the lower quadrant of Fig. 5.1, an employment function shows the relationship between the level of output and the amount of employment necessary to produce it. Thus, it also shows by how much employment will change for any given change in output. Because we are dealing with the short run where at least one factor is assumed to be in fixed supply, the shape of the curve shows that increasingly large additions to employment are necessary in order to secure any given increase in output. Diminishing returns apply. Notice that we have not said anything precise about what is meant by 'full employment'. The employment function merely states the physical relationship between the amount of labour and the amount of output. Whether the labour is available, and at what price, and whether it is actually profitable for employers to hire it at the going price, is ignored in this analysis. We just assume there are 'spare resources'. This is what is meant by some economists when they say that Keynesians have tended to take too simple a view of the labour market. We shall return to this criticism in section 7.4.

5.4 The multiplier

The multiplier effect we have just observed is a ratio. In our example it is the ratio of the eventual change in income (and of course total expenditure, ΔY, to the initial change in government spending, ΔG. Thus we can write:

$$\text{multiplier (k)} = \Delta Y : \Delta G, \text{ or } = \frac{\Delta Y}{\Delta G}$$

In fact, although we have here encountered the multiplier as a consequence of a change in government spending, it will operate whenever there is a change in 'autonomous' expenditure. By 'autonomous' we mean any component of expenditure which does not itself depend upon the level of income. In our equation listing the components of aggregate demand, the autonomous elements are I, G, and X. In the widely used 'circular flow of income' model, these autonomous expenditures are usually referred to as 'injections' into the circular flow, again, because they are assumed not to depend upon or to originate within the flow of income itself. It should, therefore, be borne in mind that our illustration of the multiplier process through its relevance to fiscal policy, could just as well be an illustration of the consequences of a change in investment spending or the demand for exports.

Assuming we have carried out the re-drawing exercise referred to in the last section, we can have no doubt that the value of the multiplier depends upon the slope of the aggregate expenditure function. In drawing it with a positive slope, we are in effect saying that there is some part of aggregate spending which is itself positively related to the level of income. That component is, of course, consumption. An absolutely essential building block of the 'Keynesian model' is the belief that 'as income increases, consumption increases but by less than the increase in income'.

So, we can say that the size of the multiplier depends upon the *slope of the consumption function*, i.e. upon the tendency for consumption to increase with increases in income. The technical expression for this is the **marginal propensity to consume** (MPC), b, which is the extra consumption resulting from the receipt of an extra until of income (i.e. $b = \Delta C / \Delta Y$). In Fig. 5.2 b is a constant since the consumption function is a straight line. Since consumption is the only part of aggregate expenditure which varies with income in this model, b is also the slope of the aggregate expenditure curve. We can see from the earlier Fig. 5.1 that the larger is b, i.e. the steeper is the aggregate expenditure curve, the greater will be the change in Y resulting from any given change in autonomous spending, I, G, or X. More precisely:

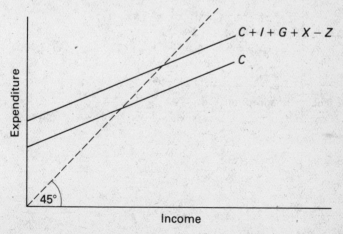

Fig. 5.2 Consumption and income

the multiplier (k) $= \dfrac{1}{1 - \text{MPC}}$

If MPC = 0.5, then k = 2; but if MPC = 0.8, then k = 5. Figure 5.3 may help us to visualise the process.

The role of the marginal propensity to consume in the multiplier is to tell us how much of an increase in one person's expenditure will be passed on by its recipient as a further addition to expenditure. In Fig. 5.3, that part which is not passed on, is referred to as saving and may be said to constitute a 'leakage'. Since, in the

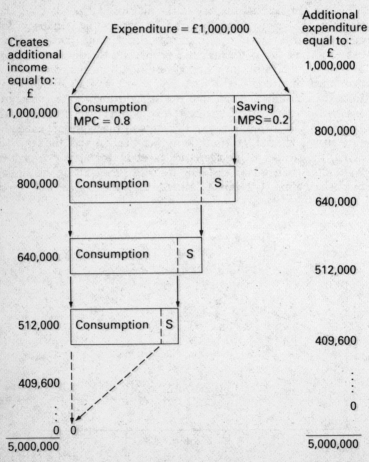

Fig. 5.3 Consumption, saving and income

simple world of Fig. 5.3, an increase in expenditure can only be either consumed or saved, if we know the value of either the marginal propensity to consume or the marginal propensity to save (MPS), we know the value of the multiplier. We can therefore regard as exact equivalents the expressions:

$$\text{multiplier (k)} = \frac{1}{1 - \text{MPC}} \text{ and } \frac{1}{\text{MPS}}$$

In practice, however, it is not true that one person's expenditure has to be either spent on domestically produced goods and services, or **saved**. When the expenditure is received as income it is likely to be **taxed**. The consumption/saving decision will therefore be based upon that part of extra expenditure which is actually received as additional post-tax or disposable income. Even then, some part of the extra disposable income which is being consumed may be used to buy **imports**. Both taxation and imports are therefore leakages which function in the same way as saving in preventing some part of extra income from being passed on as further expenditure and income. They will therefore have the same impact on the multiplier as the marginal propensity to save. An increase in the marginal propensity to tax (MPT) or the marginal propensity to import (MPM) or the marginal propensity to save will *reduce* the marginal propensity to consume domestically produced goods and services and therefore the size of the multiplier effect. One version of an expanded multiplier, incorporating all three leakages is:

$$\frac{1}{1 - [\text{MPC}\,(1 - \text{MPT})] + \text{MPM}}$$

where: MPC = marginal propensity to consume
MPT = marginal propensity to tax
MPM = marginal propensity to import
(1 − MPT) = disposable income

To conclude this discussion of the multiplier, we shall look at some illustrations using hypothetical figures.

The first benefit of this is that we can see clearly the effect upon the value of the multiplier of including the additional leakages of taxation and imports. If we take the simpler multiplier expression and put MPC = 0.8 (a reasonable figure in the light of UK data) we have

$$\frac{1}{1 - \text{MPC}} = \frac{1}{1 - 0.8} = \frac{1}{0.2} = 5$$

Still taking realistic figures we can now incorporate the marginal propensity to tax (say = 0.25) and the marginal propensity to import (say = 0.3). Now we have

$$\frac{1}{1 - [0.8\,(0.75)] + 0.3} = \frac{1}{1 - 0.6 + 0.3} = \frac{1}{0.7} = 1.4$$

Although we have used nothing but realistic figures the multiplier's value has fallen dramatically from 5 to 1.4.

A second benefit of this exercise is that it explains the seeming paradox between the very large multiplier values which one encounters in the introductory study of macroeconomics and the values which appear in models of the 'real' economy used by the Treasury and the National Institute of Economic and Social Research. It is not that either side is choosing wildly different values for the marginal propensity to consume (many texts use 0.8, and professional economists would accept values if anything slightly higher). The explanation is of course that the professional models have more complex formulations of the multiplier reflecting the more complex real world which they are endeavouring to represent.

A third benefit of introducing some quantification is to enable us to carry out, with a little more precision, the policy we instituted in section 5.3. The object, let us recall, was to raise Y to its full employment level, Y_f, by an increase in government spending. Let us assume:

Y = 22,000 bn
Y_f = 25,000 bn
MPC = 0.8
MPT = 0.25
MPM = 0.3

First of all we find the required change in the level of income. This is given by $Y_f - Y$ and equals 3,000 bn. To find now the stimulus from government expenditure required to produce this result we need to calculate a value for the multiplier. The figures given above are the same as those we used in the last calculation and that gave us a value for the multiplier of 1.4. All that remains is to divide 3,000 bn by 1.4 and we have the amount by which government expenditure must be increased to achieve our objective. The answer is 2,143 bn. These three steps are summarised below:

1. $Y_f - Y$ = 25,000 bn − 22,000 bn = 3,000 bn = ΔY

2. $\text{multiplier} = \dfrac{1}{1 - [0.8(0.75)] + 0.3} = 1.4$

3. $\Delta Y = \Delta G \times \text{multiplier} \therefore \Delta G = \dfrac{\Delta Y}{\text{multiplier}}$

$= \dfrac{3{,}000 \text{ bn}}{1.4} \simeq 2{,}143 \text{ bn}$

5.5 Changes in taxation

The first thing we can say about tax changes is that they influence income and output in a direction which is the opposite of changes in government expenditure. Other things being equal, an *increase* in taxation will reduce the level of income; a reduction in taxation will *raise* the level of income (if there is spare capacity) or prices (if there is not).

Consider the case above, where the object of fiscal policy is to increase the level of demand and output, but now let us suppose that the government endeavours to do this through a tax stimulus. The simplest form of such a stimulus is one where the government reduces its tax revenue at some particular level of income. In practice it may do this by raising the income thresholds at which the various rates of income tax become due, keeping the rates of tax and government spending constant. The effect of this is to increase consumers' disposable income. The ultimate effect upon aggregate demand, just as in the case of an increase in government expenditure, will depend upon the size of: firstly, the initial increase in spending; and secondly, the multiplier. For this reason it is tempting to think that it matters little whether the stimulus we require comes from an increase in government spending or from a reduction in taxation. Certainly, an increase in spending of 2,143 bn has the same initial effect upon the government's budgetary position as a reduction in tax revenue of the same amount. The eventual impact of these alternatives upon aggregate demand does, however, differ crucially.

5.6 The balanced budget multiplier

We must remember that the projected increase in government spending of 2,143 bn was the result of requiring an ultimate increase in income of 3,000 bn and dividing this figure by a multiplier value of 1.4. A tax remission of 2,143 bn however, is *not* equivalent to an increase in spending of the same amount. There is no mystery about this: a tax remission is simply not in itself an increase in anyone's spending. It is an *increase in disposable income* from which *some* extra spending may result but we know that some part of any increase in income will be saved. The sum to which the multiplier should be applied in this particular case is that proportion of the tax remission which is in fact spent by consumers. This will depend upon the marginal propensity to consume out of an increase in disposable income.

We are now able to compare the ultimate effect upon income of an increase in government spending with a reduction in taxation. Note that the change in taxation has to be preceded by a 'minus' sign. Remember, an increase in taxation causes a reduction in income: a reduction in taxation causes an increase.

$$\Delta Y = \Delta G \times \text{multiplier}$$
$$\Delta Y = \text{MPC} \times (- \Delta T) \times \text{multiplier}$$

An interesting and very significant consequence follows from this. Changes in government spending have a greater impact upon aggregate demand than do changes in taxation. It therefore follows that equal changes in expenditure and taxation in the same direction will *not* cancel each other out. This is the phenomenon known as the **balanced budget multiplier**. Using the figures with which we are already familiar, we can ask 'what would be the effect upon income of an increase in government expenditure of 2,143 bn accompanied, so as to maintain the existing budget balance, by an increase in tax revenue of 2,143 bn?'. The answer is that the net effect upon aggregate income will be còmposed of two contrasting influences. On the one hand, we shall have: the expansionary effect of the increase in government expenditure × the multiplier. On the other, we shall have: the contractionary tendency of the reduction in consumer spending × the multiplier. We can set this out as follows:

$$\Delta Y = (\Delta G \times \text{k}) - (\text{MPC} \times \Delta T \times \text{k})$$
$$\Delta Y = (2,143 \text{ bn} \times 1.4) - (1,714 \text{ bn} \times 1.4)$$
$$\Delta Y = 3,000 \text{ bn} - 2,399.6 \text{ bn} = 600.4 \text{ bn}$$

If we push this point to its logical conclusion we can even give a value to this balanced budget multiplier. We do this, just as we did for earlier multipliers, by dividing the ultimate change in income by the change in government spending which brought it about. Dividing 600.4 bn by 2,143 bn gives a result of 0.28.

5.7 Some difficulties with fiscal policy

There is a danger in all that we have said above, namely, that we make stabilisation look easy. Apparently, all that is necessary for governments to achieve any desired level of output (presumably a full employment level of output) is firstly to estimate the *difference* between the desired level of output and the likely level, given current policies; then to divide the difference by the multiplier, and order the required change in government spending or taxation. In fact, as Table 5.2 shows, since 1964 the growth of GNP and the

Table 5.2 Fluctuations in the rate of growth of GDP and the level of unemployment 1965–84

Year	% △ GDP*	% Unemployment
1965	2.4	1.5
1966	2.3	1.6
1967	2.5	2.5
1968	3.0	2.5
1969	1.6	2.4
1970	2.0	2.6
1971	2.6	3.8
1972	1.6	3.4
1973	8.2	2.2
1974	−1.5	—†
1975	−0.6	4.8
1976	3.9	5.5
1977	1.0	5.9
1978	3.0	5.5
1979	1.8	5.3
1980	−1.8	7.9
1981	−0.9	10.8
1982	1.4	12.2
1983	3.5	12.3‡
1984	2.4	13.1

* % change on previous year.
† Figures not available due to industrial action.
‡ Unemployment percentages after 1982 are not directly comparable with preceding years.
Source: Economic Trends, (various issues)
HMSO Tables 6, 36

level of unemployment have both shown considerable fluctuations. This has led some critics of Keynesian stabilisation policy to argue that the economy would have been better off without it.

While not wishing to agree with this view, we have to recognise a number of difficulties which make accurate stabilisation hard to achieve.

Forecasting

There is a problem of forecasting. As we just noted, the essence of successful stabilisation is that government intervention should be able to increase the level of total expenditure if it looks likely to fall short of the full employment level, and to reduce it if it looks likely to overshoot. Two critical magnitudes have obviously to be forecast. The first of these is the 'full employment potential output' of the economy at some point in the future. Since the productivity of the economy tends to rise over time, we can be certain that the maximum potential output will be greater in the future than it is now. But by how much? A good starting point for an answer might be the most recent figure for *actual* productivity growth. If we knew the most recent rate, we could at least project that into the near future. Like all statistics, however, even the most recent figures for productivity growth are 'historic'. By the time they are available to decision-makers, they refer to a strictly past trend; the trend may still be continuing but we cannot know from the figures. Even if it is, there is no guarantee that the trend will be maintained into the future.

A similar problem exists with the likely level of future demand and output on current policy settings. For us to be sure that our forecast is reliable, we need to know that our model of the economy – linking current policy settings with a particular level of demand – is accurate and that there are going to be no sudden 'shocks' to the economy. If, for example, events in the Middle East lead to a sudden rise in oil prices in six months' time, then the level of UK demand could well be less than that currently forecast. Consequently any planned intervention to (say) raise the level of demand will be insufficient to produce the full employment level. Another source of forecasting difficulty lies much nearer home. In section 5.2.3 we discussed the instability of private sector investment. If current forecasts suggest a 10 per cent shortfall in the level of demand necessary to ensure future full employment and the government pursues a compensatory fiscal policy, then the future level of demand will 'overshoot' if there is in the meantime a revival of business confidence.

Time lags

There is a problem of time lags. We can best appreciate this if we think of the sequence of stages through which policy and then action have to pass. We start with a **recognition lag**. This is the time that elapses between the economy moving in a particular direction, into recession for example, and the government becoming aware of this fact. There is a lag, probably in excess of six months, because the information upon which recognition is based, such as statistics for unemployment and industrial production, take time to collect and because a sequence of consecutive readings is necessary before a definite trend can be identified.

The recognition lag is followed by a **decision lag** while policy-makers decide upon the best course of action. To some extent, this will involve a technical discussion about whether to stimulate the economy through a tax cut or an increase in government spending or both, but in a representative democracy, where governments have to submit themselves to periodic election, the decision-making process is going to involve also a reference to the public will and to the ideological preferences of the party in government.

Decisions, having been made, take time to implement. Here is a third source of delay called the **execution lag**. If the decision has been to reduce taxes, new tax tables will have to be drawn up and sent to employers. At the same time, local tax offices will issue new codes to employees. Using the codes in conjunction with the tables, employers will eventually be able to make the smaller deductions and employees will eventually have an increase in their disposable incomes. Similar considerations apply in the case of an increase in government spending. The spending has to be spending upon something in particular. Contrary to popular prejudice, public authorities cannot just spend and have nothing to purchase. Carrying the expenditure through takes time, particularly in the case of capital projects where consultants may be involved in the planning process, public enquiries might have to be held and eventually contractors hired to carry out the work. Indeed, the time lags associated with changes in public expenditure partly explain why in practice it has been changes in taxation which have been the more favoured way of 'fine-tuning' the economy. We shall look at some other possible reasons for this below after we have examined the remaining time lags.

Even when implemented, the decision may take time to have its full effect on the economy. The increase in demand may, at least initially, only encourage retailers, wholesalers and producers to run down stocks of goods which had previously accumulated. There may still be some two to three months to wait before they become sufficiently confident of the upturn that they are prepared to take the risks of expanding production and hiring more labour. This is the **response lag**.

In short, therefore, the gap between the economy entering a particular phase and the eventual impact of a policy designed to offset it could be considerable, certainly well in excess of a year. This obviously creates the potential danger that by the time policy begins to work the economy has actually (although as yet unknown to anyone) embarked upon another phase. If this second phase is the opposite of the first, we have the obvious possibility that government policy has begun to reinforce rather than counteract the fluctuations. It has become 'destabilising'.

Changes in fiscal policy

A further difficulty with fiscal policy, quite apart from the problems of forecasting and time lags, is the possibility that frequent changes in fiscal policy will lead to *inefficiency in resource allocation*. This is an argument which has its origins in the point we made earlier, namely that changes in public expenditure have to be changes in expenditure on something in particular. There are large areas of public spending which are simply not suitable for frequent revision in accordance with the needs of stabilisation policy. Law and order and defence are two which readily spring to mind. But education and the national health service are also areas where efficient resource allocation should be based upon the health and age distribution of the population rather than upon the needs of macroeconomic policy. The nationalised industries, too, find it at best inconvenient and at worst irrational to have their long-term iunvestment plans speeded up or slowed down for reasons which have nothing to do with the market demand for their output. It may also be true, as we suggested in section 5.2.3, that frequent changes in fiscal stance make it difficult in the short run for the private sector to plan investment projects efficiently, and in the long run erode the general level of business confidence.

Political constraints

A further difficulty relates to the fact that the origin of the public sector, be it large or small, lies in an expression of public will. Namely that certain vital services should be provided by the state and be paid for via taxation, in preference to these services being provided privately and paid for at the point of consumption. Governments cannot ignore the fact that certain standards are expected to accompany the provision of these services and that consequently expenditure upon them cannot be varied over an infinite range just to meet the needs of stabilisation policy.

Financing public expenditure

An obvious, and very topical, difficulty facing fiscal policy has yet to be mentioned. Varying either the level of government spending or the level of taxation (or both) for stabilisation purposes means inevitably that government revenue and expenditure will balance only by chance. Indeed, since 1945, the UK government budget has always been in deficit. We must consider, therefore, how such deficits are to be financed and what, if any, constraints this imposes upon the conduct of fiscal policy. It is with this problem that we begin the next chapter.

Further reading

The way in which changes in taxation and government spending affect the level of aggregate demand is well explained in many macroeconomics textbooks. Stanlake (1984) Chs 9 and 20 and Lipsey (1983) Ch. 43 are examples. Black (1980) Ch. 9 analyses the effects of fiscal changes using a multiplier which incorporates all leakages but some students may find it heavy going. The same is true of Morris (1984) Ch. 13.

A very readable account of the difficulties involved in the operation of stabilisation policy generally is in Vane and Thompson (1985) Ch. 7. Chapter 5 of the same book discusses the objectives of stabilisation policy, and is, in effect, a Keynesian view of what tends to go wrong in the absence of intervention and why therefore it is necessary. The difficulties, aims and objectives are also discussed in Morris (1984) Ch. 9 and in Griffiths and Wall (1984) Ch. 25.

Factual detail on the recent conduct of fiscal policy is always included in Prest and Coppock, in the 1984 edition in Ch. 3, and a spring issue of the monthly publication *Economic Trends* always has a summary of the budget and review of 'recent developments and prospects' for fiscal policy. Savage (1982) summarises the conduct of fiscal policy between 1974 and 1981, a period which saw a movement away from traditional Keynesian ideas of stabilisation. The Treasury's *Economic Progress Reports* also contain frequent articles on fiscal matters while the most detailed and recent figures can be found in *Financial Statistics*. Griffiths and Wall (1984)

Chs 13 and 14 provide the best current survey of the composition and size of government revenue and expenditure.

Questions

*: Answers to these questions are discussed in Part II.

1. 'The consumption function is essential to the theory of income determination.' Discuss. (Oxford & Cambridge, June 1980)

2. Discuss the relationships between unemployment and government expenditure. (London, June 1982)

3.* Explain how a reduction in government expenditure, other things being equal, might affect the level of output. What difficulties are there in reducing government expenditure? (London, Jan. 1984)

4. How does fiscal policy operate to influence demand in the economy? Contrast the role of fiscal policy under Mrs Thatcher's government with its role under previous governments. (JMB, June 1982)

5.* Why is the level of aggregate private investment unstable? (London, June 1983)

Chapter Six
Government borrowing and monetary conditions

6.1 Introduction

For many years, and therefore in many textbooks, fiscal policy and monetary policy have been treated as largely separate issues. The impression given is that governments wishing to increase their expenditure without increasing their tax revenue should simply go ahead and do so, there being no need to worry about 'where the money comes from'. In a monetary economy, that is to say one in which trade is carried out via the medium of money rather than barter, this is obviously absurd. Expenditure cannot take place without money. Government departments may, of course, obtain goods on credit just like anyone else but sooner or later these goods have to be paid for and they have to be paid for with money. If this money is not forthcoming from tax revenue, it has to be raised by borrowing. As we shall see below (in sect. 6.3 and 6.4) the means by which it is borrowed may have significant effects upon both the rate of expansion of the money supply and the level of interest rates: that is, upon precisely those variables which are usually regarded as part of monetary policy.

Because of these implications for monetary policy, the size of the budget deficit and the means by which the government finances that deficit may be regarded as further constraints upon fiscal policy. How seriously governments view these constraints depends upon two things. It depends firstly upon the impact of government borrowing upon monetary conditions. If, for example, it is believed that modest deficits have a large effect upon the growth of the money stock or upon the level of interest rates, then governments will be much more concerned about their borrowing needs than if the impact is thought to be small. But this cannot be all we need to know. To make the financing of public sector deficits a serious constraint upon fiscal policy, we need to know, secondly, that these monetary conditions affect the economy in some way which matters. In the last chapter, for example, we accepted that the level of interest rates might have some influence on the level of investment spending; interest rates may also affect the exchange rate. Some economists would argue that the rate of growth of the money stock influences a wide range of expenditures, with serious consequences for the rate of inflation.

Governments of the last ten years have, in fact, shown much more concern about the size of their deficits, and about how these deficits are financed, than did their predecessors. In other words, the financing of the deficit has indeed been treated as a constraint upon fiscal policy. For Conservative governments since 1979, this constraint has been so severe that the level of public expenditure has been treated as an essential feature of, and subservient to, the apparent requirements of monetary policy. The argument behind this treatment of public spending runs briefly as follows:

1. Inflation is the most serious problem facing the UK economy;
2. Other things being equal, the rate of inflation is determined by the rate of increase in the money stock;
3. Government borrowing either adds to the money stock or raises interest rates above what they would otherwise be;
4. 'High' interest rates diminish private sector investment;
5. Private sector investment is preferable to public sector investment;
6. Therefore, government borrowing needs to be set at a level consistent with the target rate of monetary growth and the desired level of interest rates.

Plainly, we have come a long way from the 'Keynesian' idea in Chapter 5 of an independent, discretionary fiscal policy aimed at the stabilisation of output and employment. We need now to examine these propositions in more detail. In this chapter, we shall concentrate on (3); (4) we shall examine in Chapter 7; (5) is a matter of ideological preference about which we can say little in a book on economics; (1) and (2) are issues which dominate Chapter 8.

6.2 The public sector borrowing requirement

The public sector borrowing requirement is composed of:

the deficit of central government
plus the deficit of local government

plus the deficit of public corporations
plus net lending by the public sector to the private sector and overseas
plus 'other transactions and receipts'.

In other words, it encompasses the borrowing requirements of the whole of the public sector. It is of some interest, perhaps, to note that the major contributor to this borrowing requirement is the central government's capital account. Its current account usually produces a small surplus.

Two points are immediately apparent from Table 6.1. Firstly, although £10 bn may sound a very large sum of money for government to be trying to borrow in 1984/5, it is not particularly large, even in nominal terms, when compared with some earlier years. In 1975/6, for example, the PSBR at £10.6 bn was larger in spite of the lower prices of that year. This was partly as the result of a deliberate policy to enlarge the government's deficit in order to combat recession (along the lines described in section 5.3 above), and partly because, in a recession, some items of government revenue automatically diminish while some items of expenditure automatically increase. We return to this point at the end of this section.

Table 6.1 Public sector borrowing requirement, £bn at current prices, 1974/5 to 1985/6

	PSBR	*GDP*	*PSBR as % GDP*
1974/5	7.9	105.4	7.5
1975/6	10.6	125.6	8.4
1976/7	8.5	144.8	5.9
1977/8	5.6	166.5	3.4
1978/9	9.3	194.4	4.8
1979/80	9.9	226.9	4.4
1980/1	12.7	250.0	5.0
1981/2	8.6	274.2	3.1
1982/3	8.9	300.8	3.0
1983/4	9.7	307.0	3.2
1983/4	9.7	323.2	3.0
1984/5	10.2	351.4	2.9
1985/6	7.5*	378.0*	2.0*

* estimate
Sources: The National Accounts (1985, HMSO) Table 1.1;
Financial Statistics, HMSO (various issues), Table 2.6

Secondly, taking PSBR figures at *nominal* or *current* prices is not, however, very sensible. Since 1974/5 prices have risen very considerably in the UK and £10.6 bn in 1975/6 in *real* terms would compare with as much as £25 bn in 1984/5. Also, some recognition has to be made of the resources available to support this government borrowing. Over the years, GDP has increased in both real and nominal terms. In other words, even a given PSBR in real terms would be making a much smaller claim upon total output and income in 1984/5 than in 1975/6. This is apparent in the third column of Table 6.1 where the PSBR as a proportion of GDP can be seen to have declined fairly steadily over the last ten years. This may come as a surprise given government's recent assertions that it is too large and given its efforts to reduce it.

Another important point needs to be made about the PSBR, namely that each year's PSBR represents *new* or additional borrowing. Although it may seem obvious, it is worth emphasising that the PSBR is not a stock of outstanding debt, which may get larger or smaller by one or two billion each year. Rather, the whole of the PSBR is a *flow* of new debt, which has to be added to the existing total of the national debt.

Lastly, we should remember that the PSBR is only partly the outcome of deliberate decisions on taxation and government spending. Because the government publishes projections for the size of PSBR it would like to see, it is easy to suppose that the government can determine its size. This is misleading. Governments can fix only tax rates, with the eventual yield depending upon the level of economic activity. Likewise, although decisions may be made on some elements of public spending, the final total will include expenditure on 'demand-determined' components such as welfare benefits. These too are influenced by the general state of the economy. The PSBR is therefore partly a *'residual'*; it should never be considered only as an instrument of policy.

6.3 PSBR and the money supply

There are several definitions of the 'money supply'. Table 6.2 lists and explains eight of them. With the exception of the narrowest measure, M0, they all include bank deposits of one form or another. Thus it follows that, on all of these definitions, if there is a change in the stock of *bank deposits* there will tend to be a change in the size of the money stock. We can only say 'tend' because it is obviously possible, if only in theory, that a given change in bank deposits is exactly offset by an equal and opposite change in some other component of the definition. In practice this is scarcely likely.

How might a change in the volume of bank deposits come about? Whatever detailed sequences of events we may care to imagine, and there are plenty of possibilities, they will all have in common one essential feature. They will each be just one particular way by which the community increases its indebtedness to the banking system. For illustration, let us take a sequence with which some people at least will be familiar. A man approaches his bank manager for a loan to buy a new car. It matters not whether he is granted an overdraft or a personal loan; what does matter is that he now has an increase in the size of his bank deposit against which he can write a cheque transferring some of that deposit to the seller of the car. If nothing else has happened, the total of bank deposits in the economy has expanded, and these deposits can be used by their owners to buy and sell goods and services.

Although the details will differ, exactly the same process is at work if the government borrows from the banking system. The government acquires the right to write cheques to pay people, such as its employees or its suppliers and *their* deposits increase as a consequence. Once we grasp this, we have understood at least the origin of a connection between government borrowing and the money supply. What we now need to do is to fill in the details. We shall start by looking more closely at this connection. Then the record of public sector borrowing and monetary growth in recent years will be considered.

Of course, *not all* government borrowing is likely to come from the banking system. This is a pity because, were it true, we should have been able to say that any given value for the PSBR was equivalent to the same increase in the money stock. The government may, for example, borrow from the general public by issuing bonds: the official expression is borrowing from 'the non-bank private sector'. It may also sell bonds to overseas holders. Thus if we start with the PSBR as a whole, we can only say that, if nothing else changes, there will be an increase in the money stock equal to:

PSBR

minus

all sources of government borrowing
outside the banking system [1]

Table 6.2 Relationships among the monetary and liquidity aggregates and their components

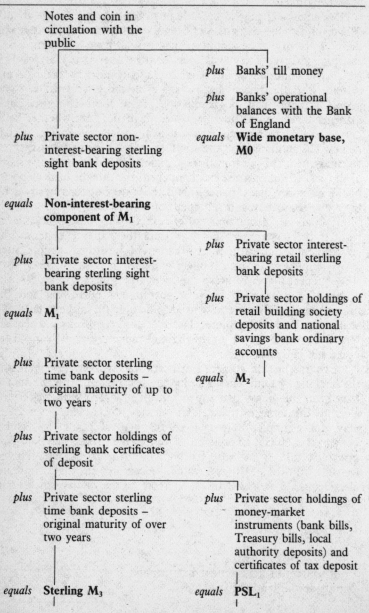

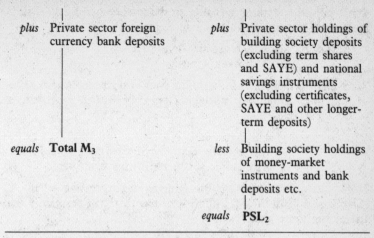

plus	Private sector foreign currency bank deposits	*plus* Private sector holdings of building society deposits (excluding term shares and SAYE) and national savings instruments (excluding certificates, SAYE and other longer-term deposits)
equals	**Total M₃**	*less* Building society holdings of money-market instruments and bank deposits etc.
		equals **PSL₂**

Source: Bank of England Quarterly Bulletin, Mar. 1984: 79.

For example, if this year's PSBR is £10 bn and, say, £7 bn is raised by borrowing from non-bank sources, then the remaining £3 bn will have to come in some form from the banking system. If nothing else changes, the money stock will increase by £3 bn.

The result of this calculation then gives us the amount of public sector borrowing that will have to be done via the banking system. Since it also gives us, at the same time, the potential increase in the money stock, this result is sometimes known as the 'monetary financing' of the PSBR. This is still not quite the end of the matter though. We have had to say several times that the amount of monetary financing will be equal to the change in the money stock, only if nothing else changes. This is simply recognising the points we made above, namely: (1) that the stock of bank deposits will be affected by private sector borrowing as well as public sector borrowing; and (2) that there are, depending on our chosen definition of money, other components which may also change in size.

If we want to relate public sector borrowing more precisely to changes in the money supply, we will need a full list of components of the money stock.

To do this requires choosing some definition from Table 6.2. One popular measure of the money stock is 'sterling M₃' which the table shows to consist of notes and coin in circulation, together with a variety of types of bank deposits. Briefly:

$$\text{Sterling } M_3 = \text{notes and coin}$$
$$+ \text{ bank deposits} \qquad [2]$$

Obviously, therefore, any change in the total of sterling M_3 will be the sum of changes in these components:

$$\Delta \text{ Sterling } M_3 = \Delta \text{ notes and coin}$$
$$+ \Delta \text{ bank deposits} \qquad [3]$$

Since there will be a change in the total of bank deposits if either or both the public and private sectors change their indebtedness to the banking system, we can rewrite [3] as:

$$\Delta \text{ Sterling } M_3 = \Delta \text{ notes and coin}$$
$$+ \Delta \text{ private sector borrowing from banks}$$
$$+ \Delta \text{ public sector borrowing from banks} \qquad [4]$$

Now, the last line of [4] is the same as the expression we met at [1] and so substituting [1] into [4] brings the PSBR explicitly into the picture once again:

$$\Delta \text{ Sterling } M_3 = \Delta \text{ notes and coin}$$
$$+ \Delta \text{ private sector borrowing from banks}$$
$$+ (\text{PSBR} - \text{all non-bank sources of}$$
$$\text{government borrowing}) \qquad [5]$$

The alternative, or 'non-bank' sources of public sector borrowing are:

(i)   sales of debt to the UK non-bank private sector
(ii) borrowing from overseas
(iii) increases in notes and coin held by the UK non-bank private sector \qquad [6]

If now we substitute [6] into [5] we have, at last, an expression which lists all possible sources of changes in our chosen definition of the money stock:

$$\Delta \text{ Sterling } M_3 = \Delta \text{ notes and coin}$$
$$+ \Delta \text{ bank lending to the non-bank private sector}$$
$$+ \text{PSBR}$$
$$- (\text{sales of debt to UK non-bank private sector} + \text{borrowing from overseas} + \text{increase in notes and coin held by the UK non-bank private sector}) \qquad [7]$$

Before we go on to look at some figures for public sector borrowing and monetary growth two further points about these accounts have to be made.

The first is easy. Notice that the change in notes and coin in circulation in effect appears twice and does so with different signs. An increase in notes and coin is plainly part of any increase in the money stock (and so we began by including it); but it is also one of the ways in which the public sector *finances* its expenditure and is therefore counted again when we include the PSBR in our expression. The two references, having opposing signs, prevents us from double counting but it also means that we could tidy the expression by cancelling them out.

The second point is more complex and more serious. These expressions which we have just developed for sterling M_3 and for changes in sterling M_3 are known as 'ex-post identities'. They tell us that any change that has occurred on one side of the equation must be matched by a change on the other side. It is because they are telling us how things are *after* the event that we use the expression 'ex-post'. The identities cannot tell us how a sequence of events will unfold *before* we initiate those events; i.e. they can tell us nothing 'causal'. Suppose, as members of the government, we agree to a reduction in PSBR of £10 bn to reduce the public sector's contribution to monetary growth. The identity [7] tells us that when the operation is complete any reduction on the right-hand side must be matched by reduction on the left. However, it cannot tell us either the size of the ultimate reduction in monetary growth, nor the sequence of events that will occur as the change works itself out. Imagine that the reduction in PSBR is achieved via cuts in government spending, and that these cuts are in aid to industry. Further imagine that because of the reduction in funds from the government, industry has to increase its borrowing from the banks. At least some part of the reduction in monetary growth is now being offset by increased private sector bank borrowing. 'At the end of the day' or 'ex-post' there is likely to be *some* reduction in monetary growth but it is not likely to be equal to the reduction in PSBR. This is because it is most unlikely that initiating a change in some single component will leave all other components undisturbed. Recognising this is enormously important for both the formulation and evaluation of policy. It means that a given desired change in the money stock cannot be brought about simply by making an *equal* adjustment to some component on the right-hand side over which the authorities happen to have some control. It also means that no quantitative change brought about by the authorities in some component on the right-hand side can ever be said to be the sole cause of what eventually transpires on the left. More will be said on this when we have looked at some recent figures for the PSBR and monetary growth in Table 6.3.

Table 6.3 PSBR, money supply and interest rates, 1974/5 to 1985/6

	(1) PSBR (£ bn)	(2) Sales of public sector debt to non- banks (£ bn)	(3) Monetary financing (= (1) – (2)) (£ bn)	(4) Change £M₃ (£ bn)	(5) (= (3)/(1)) (%)	(6) (= (3)/(4)) (%)	(7) Interest rate on 20-year bonds
1974/5	7.9	4.2	3.7	2.7	47	137	14.39
1975/6	10.6	5.3	5.3	2.4	50	221	14.43
1976/7	8.5	7.2	1.3	2.7	15	48	12.73
1977/8	5.6	6.6	–1.0	6.2	—	– 16	12.47
1978/9	9.3	8.5	0.8	5.3	9	15	12.99
1979/80	9.9	9.2	0.7	6.4	7	11	13.79
1980/1	12.7	9.3	3.4	9.0	27	38	14.75
1981/2	8.6	7.5	1.1	7.8	13	14	12.88
1982/3	8.9	10.5	–0.6	9.5	—	– 6	10.81
1983/4	9.7	9.2	0.5	9.8	5	5	10.69
1984/5	10.2	15.6	–5.4	12.9	—	– 42	10.70
1985/6	7.5*	7.0*	0.5*	14.5*	6.7*	3	10.10

Sources: CSO; *Financial Statistics,* (various issues), Tables 2.6, 11.1
* estimate

It is apparent that both the size of the PSBR and the growth of sterling M_3 have fluctuated considerably over the years. The pattern of fluctuation does not, however, appear to confirm the often heard anxiety that a large PSBR encourages rapid monetary growth. In 1975/6, for example, when the PSBR was very large (col. 1), monetary growth (col. 4) was at its smallest. In 1981/2 the position is reversed; a comparatively small PSBR is associated with rapid monetary growth. This confirms what we have been saying above: it is *not the size* of the PSBR that potentially affects monetary growth, but *the way* in which it is financed. Column 3 gives the amount of monetary financing year by year and col. 6 expresses this as a proportion of total monetary growth. In 1975/6 the monetary financing of the PSBR does appear to be related to the monetary growth that took place, being equal in fact to twice the growth in sterling M_3. Since then, monetary financing has been a very small and rather erratic proportion of the change in sterling M_3.

It is worth glancing at col. 5 which shows monetary financing as a proportion of PSBR. If one were legitimately worried about the monetary implications of a large PSBR, it would have to be, given what we have said above, because large PSBRs tend to be associated with monetary financing. In fact, there is no obvious relationship between the size of the PSBR and the proportion of it financed by monetary means. If anything, the proportion of it financed in this way has tended to fall in recent years even when the PSBR has been growing. Taking the period as a whole, there have been substantial variations in the proportion of PSBR financed by monetary means. Similar conclusions have been arrived at by more rigorous methods of testing (Savage 1980).

In summary, we can say from the figures that in practice a large PSBR does not mean a large amount of monetary financing; even if it did, this would be no guarantee of rapid monetary expansion. What this erratic association between PSBR and changes in the money stock reveals, is that the behaviour of other components in the money supply are very important. This is most clearly seen in years (such as 1981/2) when a small PSBR is associated with rapid monetary growth. Further examination of the figures would show a very rapid increase in bank lending to the non-bank private sector. In spite of government preoccupation with the PSBR, as we said at the outset, monetary growth is the outcome of bank lending to both public and private sectors and in many years the latter has dominated. In fact, much closer correlations exist between monetary growth and bank lending to the non-bank private sector than exist between monetary growth and the size of PSBR (Hall 1983: 94).

6.4 PSBR and interest rates

At the beginning of this chapter we said that the argument over public spending involved the proposition:
> government borrowing either adds to the money stock or raises interest rates above what they would otherwise be.

If, as seems to be the case, large PSBRs do not necessarily mean large amounts of monetary financing, this can only be because the monetary authorities, the Treasury and the Bank of England, have been successful in financing the borrowing requirement in other ways – for example, by selling debt to the non-bank private sector. From here it is a short step to argue that if the community has been persuaded to increase its holdings of public sector debt year by year, this can only be because the rate of interest or 'yield' on that debt has increased, so making it more attractive. If the view is then taken that private sector investment is sensitive to the level of interest rates, then it must be the case that debt sales 'crowd out' private sector spending through their effect upon interest rates.

What evidence is there for the view that if public sector borrowing does not expand the money stock it must raise interest rates? Table 6.3 is again relevant, in particular col.2 which shows the quantity of debt sold to the non-bank private sector and col.7 which shows the level of interest rates on long-dated government bonds. Since 1975/6 bond rates have fallen, though the course has not been smooth. At the same time, though again with fluctuations, debt sales have increased. Most importantly for the present argument, the very large debt sales of recent years (1982/3 to 1984/5) have coincided with nominal interest rates at their lowest for more than ten years. It is worth noting too, that for most of that period *real* interest rates (nominal rates minus the expected rate of inflation) have actually been negative.

On the face of it, therefore, large annual sales of debt have not been accompanied by steadily rising interest rates; neither have the years of particularly large sales been years of high interest rates. But before we dismiss entirely the argument that financing the PSBR by non-monetary means is detrimental to the private sector, there are two points to consider.

The first is that if one is determined to assert the evils of recent levels of government borrowing, then it is still possible to argue that whatever the level of interest rates has actually been, in the absence of such debt sales it would have been lower. Arguments of this kind have the obvious merit that they can never be disproved; on the other hand, neither can they be confirmed. All one can say is that to believe that more investment would have taken place had government borrowing been less in recent years, one has to believe that private sector investment has been inhibited by the failure of real interest rates to be even more negative than they have actually been for much of the period.

Secondly, we shall see in the next section that some part of the success in selling debt without obvious interest rate consequences, is the result of changes in the type of debt offered and the way in which it is marketed. Some of these changes involve exploiting the special privileges available only to public sector debt and available therefore only to the government as a borrower and not to the private sector. The preferential capital gains tax treatment of government stock is an example. In so far as successful debt sales are exploiting the government's privileged position, then the private sector may still find itself at a disadvantage in competing for funds.

6.5 Recent developments in debt management

We shall start by looking at what is sometimes called 'marketable debt'. This is debt for which a secondary market exists in the sense that members of the public can buy and sell the debt between themselves. Most government bonds belong to this category and are what people mean by the expression 'gilt-edged stock'. A consequence of the debt being marketable is that its price can fluctuate. It is the prices of the components of this debt that appear in the financial pages of many newspapers.

6.5.1 New types of stock

Since 1977, four new types of stock have become available.

1. In 1977 the public was first able to subscribe to a *'partly-paid'* stock by making an initial payment followed by two further instalments, usually within three months. Many partly-paid issues have since been made, their success resting on people's being able to buy them at a time when they are temporarily short of sufficient liquid funds to buy them outright.

2. Also introduced in 1977, but rather less successful, have been the issues of *variable-rate* stock.
3. In 1982 *index-linked* stocks were made available to all purchasers, having initially been restricted to pension funds and life insurance companies.
4. Also since 1982 the authorities have issued a number of *low-coupon*, *short-dated* stocks which offered subscribers a relatively low yield, but the certainty of a capital gain at the time of redemption. Since British government stock is free of capital gains tax, this low-coupon/short-date combination could be said to be exploiting one of the most distinctive features of marketable public sector debt.

6.5.2 Methods of selling debt

All of these innovations in the type of stock on offer have to be seen against a significant change also in the method of selling. Before 1979, the invariable practice was to offer stock for sale at an announced price, predetermined to make the stock attractive given current market conditions. If this fixed price failed to clear the stock, the Bank of England would be left with the unsold stock and would subsequently release it on to the market as and when conditions suggested the price would be acceptable. This was known as the 'tap' method of selling. Since 1979, the authorities have moved toward a *'partial-tender'* system where stock is announced for sale by tender, allowing the market to fix the price which will clear the stock. This is subject to a minimum tender price (hence partial-tender) designed to prevent a sudden collapse of stock prices in the event of the authorities miscalculating the timing and attractiveness of the sale. The main argument in favour of such a system is that if the price is set realistically, the authorities can be certain of selling given quantities of debt at pre-determined intervals. This certainty should allow a closer correlation of non-bank borrowing with expenditure and thus reduce the need for monetary financing.

6.5.3 National Savings

The expression 'non-marketable debt' refers to what is more popularly known as National Savings. Unlike government stock, the assets which people acquire from National Savings cannot be bought and sold between members of the public. The assets in question include National Savings certificates, deposits with the

National Savings Bank, deposits accumulated via the 'save-as-you-earn' scheme and even holdings of premium bonds. Although National Savings instruments are less frequently thought of as a means of financing the public sector's deficit than are marketable stocks and bonds, National Savings have made an important contribution in recent years. In 1981/2, net sales of non-marketable debt amounted to nearly 40 per cent of the PSBR compared with about 5 per cent in the mid 1970s. The main innovations are well known. The introduction of *index-linked, save-as-you-earn* facilities and the extension of eligibility for ownership of *index-linked National Savings certificates* have been spectacular successes but their growth has been very closely paralleled by deposits in the *National Savings Bank investment account* which, since 1977, has offered a near-money-market rate of interest in return for one month's notice of withdrawal.

Whether the authorities' ingenuity in finding new forms of debt attractive to the non-bank private sector will continue, one cannot know. It is of course possible that at some future point the remarkable depth of the UK market for public sector debt will be reached. None the less, arguments which stress the undesirable monetary consequences of a given size of PSBR have to be based upon what, in fact, has actually happened.

The doubtful wisdom of attaching so much importance to the PSBR in the conduct of macroeconomic policy is neatly summed up by Hall (1983:96).

Despite the public utterances of the government, one may conclude that the nature of the relationships between discretionary fiscal policy and the PSBR on the one hand and between the PSBR, interest rates and changes in £M$_3$ on the other, are so complex as to deny to the authorities the ready availability of a simple rule of thumb that indicates how fiscal policy should be adjusted so as to ensure that the size and structure of the PSBR remain compatible with the stated monetary target. This poses an almost unbearable burden on practitioners who seek to use the PSBR ... as a flexible instrument of monetary control, even in the medium to long-term.

Further reading

The connection between PSBR, monetary growth and interest rates is now discussed in a number of sources. Howells and Bain (1985) Ch. 4 discuss both the accounting relationships as well as looking at recent figures. Hall (1983) has two excellent Chapters, 7 and 8, on the thinking behind setting PSBR targets and the experience of trying to achieve them. Craven (1984) Ch. 18 is less concerned with the recent record but discusses the whole question of borrowing and the money supply in a helpful way.

At a more advanced level, Llewellyn *et al.* (1982) Chs 3 and 8 look at both theory and recent practice and discuss at some length the difficulties of influencing monetary growth and interest rates via the PSBR. Glynn (1983) reviews the 'Keynesian' role of public expenditure in a recession and discusses the wisdom of recent attempts to reduce the level of borrowing.

Two periodical publications which provide up-to-date figures and commentary are the *National Institute Economic Review* and the *Midland Bank Review* which carries an 'Annual Monetary Review'.

Questions

*: Answers to these questions are discussed in Part II.

1.* 'Government borrowing is the enemy of employment in two ways. First, government borrowing is inflationary which destroys confidence in the private sector. Secondly, government expenditure "crowds out" private expenditure.' Discuss. (AEB, Nov. 1983)

2.* What determines public sector borrowing and what is its relation to the money supply? (ICMA, Nov. 1983)

3.* 'The quantity of money, the rate of interest and the public sector borrowing requirement.' Discuss the argument that a government can control any two of these but only at the expense of losing control over the third. (ICSA, 1982)

4. Explain in detail how an increase in government borrowing influences:
   (a) the money supply
   (b) conditions in the money markets.
   (I of B, April 1982)

Chapter seven

Monetarism and supply-side economics

7.1 Introduction

Everyone knows that monetarism is a body of economic thought which thinks that 'money matters', that is to say, that changes in the size of the stock of money in circulation will have a significant impact on the workings of the economy. Monetarists are therefore seen as those who support such a body of doctrine. Later we shall see that this is too narrow a view and that monetarists tend to share in common a number of other views, particularly regarding the size and role of the public sector.

The substance of the monetarist view can be summarised as follows. Changes in the supply of money *inevitably* mean changes in the amount of expenditure in the economy. Changes in expenditure, if they differ from the natural rate of growth of the economy, cause changes in the general level of prices rather than in the level of output and employment. If changes in expenditure can only produce changes in prices rather than quantities, it then follows that nothing that governments can do by way of fiscal or monetary policy can have any lasting effect upon output and employment. Aggregate supply is fixed and is unaffected by changes in aggregate demand.

This is in total contrast, we must remember, to the view we developed in Chapter 5. There we showed that changes in expenditure *could* cause changes in employment and output (see Fig. 5.1 for example), and that governments should deliberately set out to create the level of expenditure which would maximise employment and output. Aggregate supply is not fixed; output and employment respond to changes in aggregate demand. In this chapter we want to examine these two contradictory propositions.

7.2 The quantity theory of money

The usual place to begin an examination of the monetarist case is with the quantity theory of money or, as it is sometimes called, the equation of exchange. This is one of the oldest ideas in economics, and can initially be summarised in the following expression:

$$M \times V = P \times T$$

which merely states that the total stock of money, M, multiplied by the number of times it is spent in a given period, V, is equal to the average price of each transaction, P, multiplied by the total number of transactions in that period, T. As it stands, this is entirely uncontroversial. Indeed, it is bound to be true since total expenditure must always equal the total value of goods and services bought. What makes the equation controversial and therefore interesting is the assertion by some economists that V and T are fixed, or change only slowly over time. If this is true, then it follows that a change in M must be reflected in a change in P. For instance, an increase in M must mean an increase in expenditure, and this increase in expenditure must mean an increase in prices rather than in the volume of trade.

By now we can see that there are two stages in the monetarist argument, each one relating to one side of the equation. On the left-hand side $(M.V)$ we have the suggestion that a change in the money stock causes a change in expenditure; on the right-hand side $(P.T)$ we have the suggestion that this change in expenditure affects prices and not quantities. We shall now consider separately each stage of the argument.

7.3 Money and expenditure

To say that an increase in the money stock must produce an increase in expenditure is to say that people have only one use for money, namely, to spend it on goods and services. This is not altogether unreasonable. It is what people mean when they say that money has no value in itself, but is useful only for what it will buy. In more technical language, money has no intrinsic value, rather its sole function is as a 'medium of exchange'; or equivalently, the transactions motive is the sole motive for holding money. Money held to support transactions in goods and services is said to constitute the community's active balances. If this is the sole motive for holding money, then clearly any change in the quantity of money in circulation will be reflected in a change in expenditure.

7.3.1 Breaking the money-expenditure link

Idle balances and the speculative motive
One obvious criticism of the left-hand side of the quantity theory expression is that some part of the money stock is held as a form of saving. Money now takes on a secondary function, it acts as a 'store of value' and is held in what is often referred to as idle balances. The motive for holding such balances is usually called the 'speculative' motive. Introducing a speculative motive opens up at least the theoretical possibility that any change in the money stock will be accommodated entirely by a change in the holding of idle balances rather than by a change in expenditure. This is precisely what happens in the famous Keynesian 'liquidity trap' case. Clearly, the quantity theory prediction relies heavily on there being only a transactions motive for holding money.

We need to appreciate that the debate about the motives for holding money is essentially a debate about velocity or V in the equation. The greater the amount of money people wish to hold, for whatever motives, the smaller the proportion of the money stock which can be circulating, i.e. the smaller is V. Because some components of the money stock (notes and coin, bank deposits and so on) are circulating, being transferred from one person to another many times in the course of a year, the year's total value of transactions can be carried out with a stock of money which is considerably smaller. In the UK at present, the total output of goods and services (represented by GDP) is about three times the size of the money stock (represented by £M_3) and thus the income velocity of circulation is said to be three.

Returning to the equation $M \times V = P \times T$, if V remains constant then any proportionate change in the money stock must result in the same proportionate change in expenditure. If indeed V were constant, then the quantity theory prediction would hold in its strongest form. But if idle balances are part of a speculative motive for holding money, then V can vary, and the simple link between money and expenditure will be broken.

Predictable changes in velocity
The quantity theory prediction would still hold, although in a weaker form, even if velocity varied, provided that the variations were *predictable*.

The most predictable influences upon velocity go under the general heading of 'institutional arrangements'. They are many and varied.

Changes in the frequency of payment. The average bank balance of a man earning as much as, say, £10,000 might be as low as £250. One of the reasons for this is that he knows he will be paid his salary in monthly instalments. The maximum he has to hold by way of ready spending power is what he needs to see him through to the next pay-day. Think of what he would have to hold if he were paid only at the beginning of the year and contrast that again with what he could manage with if only he were paid weekly. Changes in the frequency of receipts and payments therefore affect velocity but since they occur only slowly and steadily they are predictable.

Changes in the availability of money-substitutes. People's need to hold money balances will depend also upon the ease and convenience with which they could obtain such balances if they suddenly needed to do so. If there are near substitutes, the demand will be lower (velocity higher) than would otherwise be the case. A very clear example of this is provided by a recent Treasury study of the demand for notes and coin (Johnston 1984). The study concluded that the demand for this part of the money stock had fallen over the last few years because of the growth of cash dispensers which meant cash balances could be more easily replenished than hitherto. Again, however, the development was gradual and the Treasury is prepared to predict future changes on the strength of recent experience.

Changes in financial institutions. Another example is provided by the rapid growth in recent years of building societies. Suppose we define the money stock to exclude building society deposits (as we do in the case of £M_3, for example). If people hold increasing quantities of building society deposits instead of money, because these pay interest and yet can be easily reconverted to money, then they are in effect raising velocity. By reducing *their* demand for money, building society depositors are making it available to others to finance additional expenditures: therefore velocity increases.

Changes in interest rates. The effect of institutional changes, probably because they are comparatively slow, is non-controversial. Much more a source of argument between economists, because changes are frequent and sometimes large, is the significance of interest rates. It seems reasonable to suppose that when interest rates are 'high' there will be a smaller demand for money (higher velocity) than when interest rates are 'low'. This is because interest is paid to holders of assets which are not normally regarded as money, although the picture has become more complicated in the last year or so as banks have begun to pay interest on certain types of instant-access deposit. Therefore, on a simple view, the rate of interest is the opportunity cost of holding ('proper') money. The higher the cost, the lower the demand. But, as with all cases of demand in economics, the strength of this relationship, measured by elasticity, will depend upon the nearness of substitutes.

Unfortunately one can never discuss the nearness of substitutes without taking, first, some prior view on the purpose of the good in question. In the case of money we are driven back to the question of just how much of money's job is to act as a medium of exchange and how much as a store of value. If the former dominates, certainly if it is the sole function, then there are probably few substitutes. In the end, purchases have to be paid for with money. There is no real substitute, recent inventions such as credit cards serving only to achieve a temporary transfer of the debt. If money is also a store of value, a useful way of holding part of one's total wealth, however, then there are plainly many substitutes, government bonds, building societies, SAYE schemes and the like. In such circumstances a small rise in interest rates might well induce a significant drop in the demand for money. Even so, let us remember, although monetarists would undoubtedly prefer the interest elasticity of the demand for money to be low and velocity to be little affected by interest rate changes, provided the effect is predictable, the quantity theory prediction will still hold.

Unpredictable changes in velocity

Although the points raised above somewhat diminish the force of the quantity theory, the real threat to the left-hand side of the equation is the possibility that velocity might be *unpredictable*. This will be true if people increase or decrease their holdings of idle balances in response to circumstances which cannot be measured or predicted. Obviously, monetarists are going to want to say that such a situation rarely if ever arises. On the other hand Keynesians contend that velocity really is unstable, largely because interest rates change frequently and people have imperfect information about the future course of interest rates.

If the rate of interest is the opportunity cost of holding money and interest rates are always greater than zero, why should people ever hold any idle balances? Why hold anything more than the minimum amount of money necessary to see one through the day, week or month? The distinctively Keynesian response is that

117

people are typically uncertain. (Perhaps it is worth recalling just how strongly this featured in our discussion of the Keynesian view of instability in section 5.2.3.) What they are uncertain about here is the future value of those assets which are near substitutes for money. The nearest substitutes are financial assets, and we know from a glance at the appropriate pages of a quality newspaper that the prices of such assets can fluctuate. The value of individual assets may fluctuate for a wide variety of reasons, of course, but the one event which will tend to push all asset prices in the same direction is a change in interest rates. A rise in interest rates makes newly created assets (carrying the new rates) more attractive than existing assets at existing rates. People will sell existing assets in order to buy new, pushing down the price of the existing stock of assets until the effective yield is as good as it is on the new. A rise in interest rates therefore entails a capital loss for holders of existing assets, whilst the reverse process will entail a capital gain.

Obviously, anyone anticipating a rise in interest rates will gain if he sells his assets *before* their price falls, and holds money instead. *After* the price fall, he will be able to buy a larger quantity of assets yielding the higher rate of interest. Conversely, the anticipation of a fall in interest rates (and rise in asset prices) should lead to a movement out of money as a store of wealth and into assets to achieve a capital gain. If everyone had perfect information regarding future interest rate movements, then obviously everyone would hold entirely money or entirely financial assets. There would never be a simultaneous demand for both. Because information is *imperfect*, however, two things follow. First, at any moment, some people will be expecting interest rates to rise, some expecting them to fall and others expecting them to remain unchanged. Depending upon the balance of numbers in these three categories, the demand for money may be high or low. It is unlikely ever to be infinite or zero. Second, even individual savers will be unsure in their own minds about the future movement of interest rates. An individual may think there is, say, a 60 per cent probability that interest rates will rise, a 10 per cent chance that they will fall, and a 30 per cent chance that they will remain unchanged. Such an individual would hold the balance of his wealth in money but might still hold some bonds against the possibility that interest rates actually fall. Once again, we may expect people to hold a *balance* between money and bonds depending on their assessment of the next likely movement in interest rates.

The frequency with which people shift their wealth between money and non-money assets, clearly depends on how they form their expectations of future interest rate movements. It seems reasonable to suggest that, other things being equal, the higher the actual rate of interest, the greater the balance of people who feel that its next most likely movement is downwards, and vice versa. At 'high' rates therefore, people will buy non-money assets, reinforcing incidentally what we earlier said about interest rate being the opportunity cost of holding money. None the less, people may be uncertain about what precisely is a 'high' rate in particular circumstances; in other words, they may be uncertain about the next likely movement in interest rates and may, even when rates appear historically 'high', rush into money because some development in the economy causes them to expect a further rise.

Let us emphasise: the greater the uncertainty about future interest rate movements the larger and more frequent the changes in the demand for money balances (and therefore in velocity) at any rate of interest. The Keynesian criticism of the left-hand side of the quantity theory expression is that people are uncertain and markets are imperfect. The typical monetarist view is that people possess good information about the markets in which they operate. They are reasonably confident therefore about future price movements. Their confidence is generally justified. Their demand for money balances (and velocity) is stable and predictable.

7.3.2 Empirical evidence

What evidence do we have regarding the interest-elasticity of the demand for money and of its stability?

There seems little room for doubt that the demand for money is *interest-elastic* and that the connection between changes in the money stock and expenditure may be weaker than monetarists would wish. Many tests have been carried out, for different countries, over different time periods, using different interest rates, definitions of income and statistical techniques. Almost all have shown a significant negative relationship between interest rates and the demand for money (Artis and Lewis 1981; Pierce and Tysome 1985).

On the *stability* or predictability of any interest rate:demand for money relationship, the picture is less clear. In the early 1970s evidence seemed to provide strong support for the monetarist argument in favour of stability (Laidler 1971). Now it appears likely that that relationship broke down during the 1970s and the demand for money function became quite unstable, especially if the definition of money used is £M$_3$ (Artis and Lewis 1981).

7.4 Expenditure and prices

In this section we want to examine the right-hand side of the quantity theory equation and the suggestion that any increase in expenditure will lead to a rise in prices rather than in the quantity of goods traded. The first step is unproblematic: we begin by assuming that there is a fixed relationship between the volume of goods and services traded, T, and the flow of newly produced goods and services. For T to increase, therefore, there must be an increase in the level of output. For Keynesians, as we saw in Fig. 5.1, this is a perfectly possible response to an increase in aggregate expenditure, at least in many circumstances; to monetarists apparently it is not. Why do we have these two apparently contradictory positions and, perhaps more important, how do we choose between them?

An obvious place to start is to say that it all depends on whether there are unemployed resources with which to produce the extra output: the Keynesian view assumes there are, the monetarist one assumes there are not. But this apparently simple solution raises the decidedly awkward question of what we mean by 'unemployment', because the quantity theory tradition has a number of influential supporters amongst economists and politicians today even when there appear to be very substantial unemployed resources in the economy.

7.4.1 Breaking the expenditure–price level link

To understand how anyone at the present time could seriously assert that there is 'full employment' in the sense required by the quantity theory, we need to look at Fig. 7.1. On the vertical axis we have the real wage rate (i.e. average money wages divided by an index of the general price level) and on the horizontal axis the level of employment. N_s depicts the supply of labour and N_D the demand for it. In Fig. 7.1 we have an equilibrium real wage, w/p, and an equilibrium level of employment, N, 'equilibrium' in the sense that at the current real wage there are no workers who wish to work but cannot find jobs and no firms wanting to hire labour but unable to find workers. Because all transactors are happy with the arrangements, the situation is sometimes described as the 'market clearing' situation of full employment. Note that this definition of 'full employment' does not yield an absolute figure. The curves could cross, and equilibrium exist, at theoretically any position along the horizontal axis. Meanwhile, what we think of as

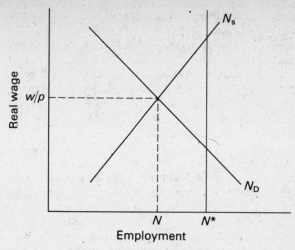

Fig. 7.1 Labour market equilibrium

the total workforce is likely to be a fixed absolute number, e.g. $N^\star$ in Fig. 7.1. Therefore, it is possible for full employment, in the market clearing sense, to leave quite a gap between the number of people in work and the number potentially available. However, since those not working do not wish to work at the current real wage they are regarded by monetarists as voluntarily unemployed. Thus, in Fig. 7.1, we could show the total number of people potentially available for work as $N^\star$ and call the difference, $N^\star - N$, 'voluntary unemployment'. The assertion that the labour market really does behave like this is, of course, controversial and we shall want to look at the arguments more closely later. For the moment, however, it is more important to realise that this is the view that has to be taken if the quantity theory is to be accepted. Only if the labour market is regarded as clearing in this way can it be argued that changes in aggregate expenditure produce no changes in output, but rather changes in prices alone – i.e. the strict monetarist contention. If the labour market does not clear in this way, then the Keynesian contention that extra aggregate demand raises output and employment, and not prices, becomes more plausible.

7.4.2 The effect of increasing expenditure

What we want to do in this section is to trace the effect of an increase in aggregate expenditure, assuming that we have an equilibrium level of employment. We shall do this by looking at the effect as experienced, firstly, by firms and then by workers. Imagine an increase in aggregate expenditure. Remember, too, that market clearing equilibrium is a general state of affairs, i.e. there are no unfulfilled desires on the part of economic agents. Immediately, we can see that it follows that firms are maximising profits producing just their current level of output, and workers are happy to provide just the current amount of labour.

The initial impact on firms

Consider the impact on an individual firm of this increase in aggregate demand. As far as the entrepreneur is concerned, there is an increase in demand for his output. He may have his suspicions, if he reads the right newspapers, that this is part of some policy to raise total spending in the economy rather than a change of consumer taste in favour of his own product, but the distinction cannot matter to him. Faced with an increase in demand for his product, a profit-maximising firm must try to increase its output. This stage of the argument can be illustrated by the familiar diagram of a perfectly competitive firm.

In Fig. 7.2, the initial effect upon an individual firm of an increase in aggregate demand is to raise the profit-maximising level of output from Q to Q'. Output apparently is responding to demand. But what about employment? Workers, we know, were content to be supplying the original volume of labour. If our entrepreneur and others like him want to hire more, they are going to have to pay a higher real wage. This they can do only by offering a higher *money* wage. Still, this does not entirely rule out some increase in employment. After all, there was an increase in demand; customers were prepared to pay a higher unit price for a greater quantity.

The eventual impact on firms

Two things unfortunately put an end to any possibility that this increase in employment might last. Remember, the increase in demand is an increase in *aggregate* demand: all firms and markets are affected. Remember also, all these markets were initially clearing. Thus, throughout the economy, firms are doing exactly as ours is doing above. But they are doing it not just for labour but for all factor inputs. They are having to bid a higher price for all inputs. If we follow this little story through to its end before reverting to a little theory, we can say that although customers

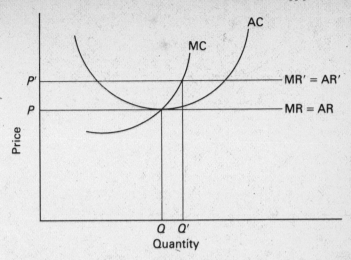

Fig.7.2 Firms and increases in demand – I

began by indicating a willingness to pay a higher price for a larger quantity, the rise in production costs means that firms have to charge the higher price for the original quantity.

Figure 7.3 shows what has happened. As we said above, the initial effect was to increase demand and the profit-maximising level of output to Q' at price P'. The cost curves of Fig. 7.2, however, were drawn on the assumption of constant money prices for any quantity of factor inputs. The fact that they are U-shaped (i.e. eventually show unit costs are rising) has nothing to do with the price of factor inputs, but is the result of the purely physical relationship expressed in the law of diminishing marginal productivity. For an individual firm, the assumption that various quantities of a factor can be bought at a constant unit price is not unreasonable, provided we assume the firm does not dominate the market for that particular factor. If all firms are trying to buy more factor inputs, however, and if the quantity of factors being supplied initially is exactly what their owners are just prepared to supply at the initial price, then clearly we cannot stay with the assumption of constant prices. In Fig. 7.3, we show the increase in input costs by the upward shift of the cost curves. The *original equilibrium quantity is restored.*

The initial impact upon workers
Now let us look at this from labour's point of view. The increase

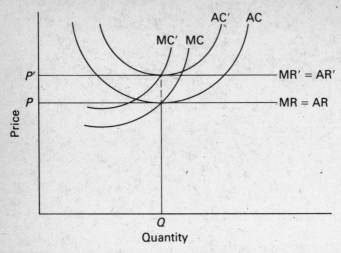

Fig. 7.3 Firms and increases in demand – II

in demand initially caused firms to try to hire more labour by offering higher money wages. Since the labour market is believed to be clearing, more labour will be forthcoming only if this money wage rise is seen as a real wage increase. That is, if workers expect prices to rise by less than the rise in wages they will move along their supply curve in Fig. 7.1.

The eventual impact on workers
But we have already established that all prices are going to rise. The increase in real wages is eroded and the supply of labour reverts to its original level.

How long all of these adjustments take to work themselves out, of course, depends upon the length of time it takes for participants to work out what is really happening. Here we encounter a difference of opinion between the 'orthodox monetarist' and 'rational expectations' schools. On an **orthodox** view it takes time for workers to realise that their increased money wages count for nothing in real terms; it takes time for individual firms to realise that all their input prices are rising. Depending on how long it takes to discover the mistake there may be some temporary increase in output and employment. But it cannot last. On a **rational expectations** view, people use their experience to be less easily fooled. If they are not fooled, there is not even a temporary effect.

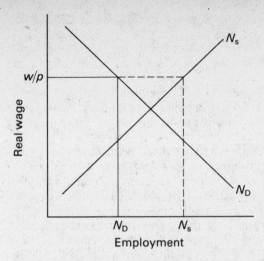

Fig. 7.4 Disequilibrium in the labour market

The Keynesian effect
In contrast to this, the Keynesian effect of an increase in expenditure is an increase in output and employment. As we said in section 7.4.1, to get this result we have to imagine a labour market in disequilibrium, as in Fig. 7.4.

At the current real wage, supply exceeds demand. There is 'involuntary' unemployment because people wish to work at the going rate but cannot find jobs; the market is not clearing. Now, if we repeat the increase in expenditure, we shall have a sequence of events very similar to that described above but with one crucial difference. Some input prices will rise and therefore the cost curves will still shift upwards. But the shift will be less than before because there will be no need to bid a higher price for labour. Figure 7.4 tells us that workers are prepared to work for a *lower* real wage. The new equilibrium position for the individual firm will lie between that of Figs 7.2 and 7.3. In aggregate, there will be some increase in employment and output, and some rise in prices.

7.4.3 Voluntary unemployment and supply-side economics

To assert that we have full employment when 3.25 m. people are successfully claiming some form of unemployment benefit needs some defending. According to the argument we considered in section 7.4.1, if we have market clearing then those without work are voluntarily unemployed. This seems, firstly, outrageous and, secondly, at odds with the facts, since many of the unemployed are actively seeking work.

To appreciate the argument at all, we have to rid ourselves of any idea that 'voluntary' refers to individual actions. It is not being said that each individual drawing unemployment or related benefit has by his own individual actions made him or herself unemployed. Rather, it is better understood to mean something like 'what society as a whole, by its collective decisions, has volunteered for'.

In Fig. 7.5, we have the labour market again, but with two supply curves. The intersection of N_s and N_D give us an equilibrium real wage and volume of employment and, just as in Fig. 7.1, we can see that there is a sizeable gap between the numbers in employment, N, and the total potential number of employees, $N^\star$. The supply curve N_s is the curve as it confronts employers; that is, it shows the number of workers available in the right place and with the right skills, for any given cost to employers. To the right of N_s, we have a 'ghost' supply curve N_s' which shows the number of workers willing to work at any given real wage, if only they were

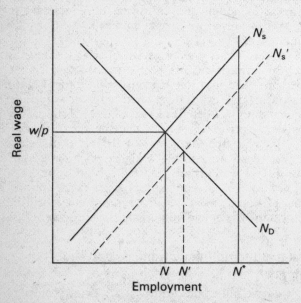

Fig. 7.5 Natural rate of unemployment

able to make the offer to employers and if the disutility of work were the only cost they had to endure. The difference between the two is caused by a number of institutional features which, depending on one's ideological preference, are called either the essential features of a humane society or 'market imperfections'. N_s' is the supply curve as it would exist in a perfectly competitive market and N' is the level of employment at which the market would then settle. Plainly there would be less unemployment ($N^\star - N'$). The difference between the actual market clearing level of employment and that theoretically attainable in a perfect market ($N' - N$) is Friedman's 'natural (or 'normal') rate of unemployment'.

What sort of influences keep the actual supply curve to the left of N_s'? National insurance contributions, employers' sick pay and maternity obligations, employment protection legislation and redundancy compensation are all costs of employing any given quantity of labour over and above the wage that has to be paid. Looked at from the workers' side, there are a number of influences which perhaps serve to reduce the supply of labour at any given real wage below what it would otherwise be. These include unemployment and related benefits which reduce the cost of being unemployed and therefore the net reward from working. Also the high monetary and non-monetary costs of moving from where jobs are short to where the chances of employment are better. In so far as these impediments to employment are the result of political decisions or personal taste, the unemployment which results is 'voluntary'.

What all this amounts to is the assertion that output and employment are fixed by the intersection of the labour supply and demand curves. If output and employment are to increase, then either the labour supply or the demand curves, or both, must shift to the right.

In recent years some economists have argued that it may be possible for governments to encourage a rightward shift of the supply curve (see pp. 72–3). This is a particularly attractive argument to those who accept the analysis of Fig. 7.5, namely, that there is a 'true' labour supply curve lying to the right of that which effectively exists in the market. To shift the actual curve towards the true one it is necessary to remove the 'rigidities' or 'market imperfections' which keep it in its present position. This involves encouraging people to be more mobile, to be more willing to retrain, and to search for work more enthusiastically. In practice, it involves increasing the penalties for not doing these things and increasing the rewards for doing them. In short, it requires an improvement in incentives.

On the negative side it is argued that incentives will be improved by reductions in the real value of welfare benefits and by weakening the power of trade unions which encourage expectations of 'unrealistic' real wages.

On the positive side, it is argued that cuts in taxes which enable people to retain more of the gains from their efforts will encourage them to do more work or to seek work.

This supply-side philosophy was summed up in the 1985 budget speech by Chancellor Lawson, in words which emphasise the difference between the Keynesian ('cut taxes to boost demand') approach and the monetarist/supply-side ('cut taxes to encourage supply') approach.

> The supply-side policy is . . . that the way to improve economic performance and create more jobs is to encourage enterprise, efficiency and flexibility; to promote competition, deregulation and free markets; to press ahead with privatisation and to improve incentives. *The argument over which will have a bigger impact on demand, increased public expenditure or lower taxation, completely misses the point. The case for lower taxation rests on supply-side policy*: lower taxes will help to enhance incentives, eliminate distortions, improve the use of resources and heighten the spirit of enterprise. (Emphasis added.)

7.4.4 The evidence

The hypothesis is virtually untestable. One cannot directly observe a supply curve, only the quantity supplied. Therefore, whether the prevailing level of employment corresponds to N in Fig. 7.5 we cannot tell. It is possible to look at changes in employment legislation and unemployment benefit to see if the volume of employment also varies as if the supply curve were moving. Thus, the introduction of earnings related supplement to unemployment benefit in 1966 might be said to have shifted the supply curve so as to account for the rise in unemployment between 1966 and 1968. Against this, however, the years of most rapid increase, 1980–83, were years in which the supplement was withdrawn, the real value of other benefits was reduced and the power of market forces was generally enhanced. There is further discussion of the evidence on incentives and labour supply in section 2.2.1.

7.5 'Crowding out'

What all this amounts to is a potentially powerful argument against the kind of government intervention in the economy that we described in Chapter 5. There, we said, governments could and should vary their own expenditure so as to push aggregate demand to the level at which all resources were fully employed, and maintain it at that level in spite of any fluctuations in private sector spending.

According to the argument in section 7.4, however, the economy is always at, or at least is moving towards, full employment, when this term is properly understood. If the economy is indeed fully employed, an increase in the public sector's demand for resources (as would occur with an expansionary fiscal policy, for example) can only be met by resources being diverted from the private sector – there cannot be any net increase in employment and output. This is known as 'resource crowding out'.

The argument in section 7.3 reinforces this idea and is the theoretical basis for the worries we discussed in sections 6.1 and 6.4 about the connection between large PSBRs and interest rates.

In section 7.3 we said that supporters of the quantity theory regarded velocity as both stable and subject only to slow change. To say that velocity is nearly constant is another way of saying that the demand for money to hold is nearly constant; that is, it does not vary much with changes in interest rates. This low interest-elasticity of demand for money is then explained by the lack of close substitutes for money, money being seen primarily as a medium of exchange.

An increase in government spending can be financed in one of three ways: by borrowing from the banking system, by an increase in taxation, and by borrowing from the non-bank private sector. The first case, since it amounts to an increase in the money stock, monetarists would of course accept as expansionary of expenditure (but not of output). It does not divert resources from the private sector; it does not 'crowd out'. On the other hand, neither is it fiscal policy, monetarists would say. It is monetary policy in thin disguise.

The second method, financing expenditure by an equal increase in taxation, crowds out private sector expenditure to the extent that the private sector reduces its expenditure to pay the extra tax. Certainly, the net increase in aggregate expenditure will be comparatively small. In section 5.6, for example, we performed a balanced budget multiplier exercise of this kind, using plausible values and found a net increase in expenditure of only 0.28 of the increase in government spending. Nearly three-quarters of the extra government spending had been offset by reductions in private spending. In fact, because of alternative theories of consumption, saving and investment which are not within the scope of this book, monetarists would give even smaller values to the balanced budget multiplier. The point is not worth arguing in the present context. An increase in government spending financed by an equal increase in taxation is not going to be very, if at all, expansionary.

This leaves us with the third possibility, that the increase in government spending could be financed by borrowing from the non-bank private sector.

As we said in section 6.4, at any particular time the general public will have its savings (its wealth portfolio) distributed among a variety of assets of differing yield, risk and maturity. If we assume, as monetarists always do, that at any time the public is also happy with this arrangement (that is, is in or is very close to port-folio equilibrium), then the question arises of how people are to be induced to buy more government debt? If we turn this question round we immediately see the importance of the demand for money. The revised question is how are people to be induced to give up some of their present holdings of the money stock, in exchange for debt? The obvious answer is that new debt has to be made more attractive and the almost equally obvious way of doing this is by offering a higher rate of interest upon the debt. By just how much the rate of interest has to be raised depends upon the interest-elasticity of the demand for money; that is, it depends upon how good a substitute for money people regard bonds. In section 7.3 we said that the characteristically monetarist view is that substitutability and therefore interest-elasticity of money demand are low. Therefore it follows that the rise in interest rates will have to be large.

Interest rates affect certain types of expenditure. There is no argument about this but, predictably, there is dispute about which classes of expenditure are involved and about their sensitivity to interest rate changes. The Keynesian view, we established in section 5.2.3, is that changes in interest rates affect mainly invest-ment but that investment is not so much sensitive to interest rates as to expectations. For monetarists, investment is sensitive to interest rate changes and so too are other categories of expenditure. Interest rates matter. Therefore, an increase in government spending financed by borrowing will cause a large rise in interest rates and this will cause a large fall in private sector spending. This is sometimes referred to as 'financial crowding out'.

As usual, the evidence is not totally conclusive. The weakest part of the financial crowding out argument is undoubtedly the assertion that government borrowing must raise interest rates significantly. This seems unlikely. In section 7.3 we noted that the evidence pointed to the demand for money being moderately interest-elastic. In section 6.4 we said there was no observable connection between interest rates and large debt sales, and in section 6.5 we offered the view that this was because, so far at least, the authorities had found other, non-interest, inducements to hold debt. We also noted that for most of the years in which interest rates had been accused of inhibiting private investment (though not at the moment) real interest rates had been exceptionally low and frequently negative.

Further reading

There is no shortage of books which explain the essential features of monetarism, though not all are at an accessible level. Beginning students will get some help from Stewart (1972) Ch. 6 and Dunnett (1982) Chs 5 and 8. An entertaining account is in Hawkins and Mackenzie (1982) Ch. 1. Those with some experience of macro-economics could probably cope with Vane and Thompson (1979), Morgan (1978) and Dow and Earl (1982) Chs 14 and 15.

A much more ambitious survey, which distinguishes varieties of monetarism, is Cross (1982) but most students will find it very tough. Almost as tough is Greenaway and Shaw (1983) but Chapters 7 and 8 deserve a mention because they deal with the labour market side of the quantity theory, an aspect of the monetarist position which is often ignored in introductory texts. See also Brown (1984).

The theme of 'crowding out' runs through several accounts of monetarism. Dow and Earl (1982) Ch. 10 is devoted to it.

On evidence, Goodhart (1984) lists all the recent tests on demand for money functions but is too advanced for any but specialists. Greenaway and Shaw (1983) Ch. 5 deal with the evidence more briefly. One of the best sources for beginners is probably Peston (1982) Ch. 7. The most recent survey is in Pierce and Tysome (1985).

The discussion about labour supply and incentives relies much more heavily upon principles (of income and substitution effects) than upon evidence. Such evidence as exists on the relevance of social security benefits is discussed by A. B. Atkinson in Creedy (1981).

Questions

*: Answers to these questions are discussed in Part II.

1.* How might government capital spending affect private sector investment? (London, June 1984)

2.* How is an increase in the money supply likely to affect the general level of prices and output? (ACA, June 1982)

3. Discuss the view that a government can moderate the rate of inflation by exercising an appropriate restraint on the rate of increase in the supply of money. (WJEC, June 1980)

4. Discuss the consequences of an increase in the supply of money. (London, June 1984)

5.* What effects will a rise in interest rates have upon: (a) business investment; and (b) the demand for money? (Oxford, June 1982)

Chapter eight
Inflation

8.1 Introduction

During the last ten years, but at an increasing rate since 1979, there has been a dramatic change in governments' conduct of economic policy. The change can be seen firstly in the objectives of policy. From 1944 to 1974, the primary objective was to minimise the level of recorded unemployment, bearing in mind the simultaneous, and sometimes conflicting, need for a sound balance of payments. Since 1974, the eradication of inflation has become the dominant, and since 1979 the overwhelming, objective.

There has been a change also in the methods of policy. Briefly, there has been a shift from short-term discretionary policy towards the use of medium-term rules and guidelines.

In this chapter (in sect. 8.2) we want to examine two theories of the inflationary process. One of these, the monetarist view, follows easily from the arguments of the last chapter and underlies the shift in policy just described. In section 8.3 we shall look at some of the supposed costs of inflation, since the belief that these are considerable is also responsible for the shift in the objectives of policy. Lastly, (in sect. 8.4) we shall look in more detail at the shift in policy, contrasting the current approach with the 'Keynesian' approach outlined in Chapter 5. Table 8.1 shows the rates at which prices have risen in recent years.

8.2 Theories of inflation

There are two approaches to the inflationary process which we want to look at. We shall call these the 'Keynesian', and 'monetarist'.

Table 8.1 Rate of change of retail
prices (% p.a.) 1963–85

1963	2.0		
1964	3.2	1975	24.2
1965	4.8	1976	16.5
1966	3.9	1977	15.8
1967	2.4	1978	8.3
1968	4.8	1979	13.4
1969	5.4	1980	18.0
1970	6.3	1981	11.9
1971	9.4	1982	8.6
1972	7.1	1983	4.6
1973	9.2	1984	5.0
1974	16.1	1985	6.0

Source: Economic Trends (various issues) HMSO,
Table 42

8.2.1 The Keynesian view of inflation

According to the Keynesian model of the economy, which we
looked at in Chapter 5, an increase in aggregate demand, at less
than full employment, would lead to higher output and employment (see Fig. 5.1). No one, least of all Keynes himself (whose
book *How To Pay For The War* (1941) was a set of instructions on
how to avoid inflation), had any doubts as to what would happen
if aggregate demand continued to rise after 'full employment' had
been reached. Eventually, there would emerge an inflationary gap
– a gap between the total money expenditure which people planned
to undertake and the total money value of full employment output
at current prices. This is shown in Fig. 8.1.

The only possible outcome of an increase in aggregate expenditure, E, beyond the full employment output level, Y, is a rise in
the market price of the goods and services produced, until their
new money value is equal to planned money expenditure.

Neither did anyone have serious doubts that the rise in prices
would begin before the figures for recorded unemployment fell to
zero. It was recognised that there would always be some frictional
unemployment and possibly some structural unemployment arising
from a geographical and skill mismatch between the unemployed
and available vacancies.

If the Keynesian theory of inflation were correct, this would lead
us to expect that as aggregate demand rose, recorded unemployment would fall and eventually prices would begin to rise. At just

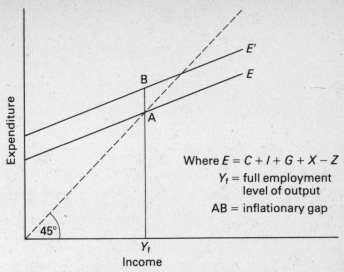

Fig. 8.1 Inflationary gap

the right moment, confirmation appeared in the shape of the Phillips curve. Looking at each year from 1861 to 1957, A.W.H. Phillips examined pairs of data composed of the percentage rate of change of money wages and the level of unemployment. The results are shown in Fig. 8.2.

The conclusion was obvious. If we were prepared to accept the level of unemployment as a measure of the pressure of aggregate demand, and the change in money wages as an indicator of changes in the general price level, then Keynes was right. As aggregate demand increases, unemployment falls until we achieve 'full employment' at somewhere between 2 and 4 per cent recorded unemployment, after which inflation becomes significant.

Note, because it is important in any comparison with the monetarist view, that an increase in, and eventual excess of, aggregate demand can come from any of its components; that is, from any one of

$$C + I + G + X - Z$$

Consumers may decide to save less, businessmen to invest more, governments to spend more on defence, foreigners to buy more of our exports or UK residents to buy fewer foreign imports. It is particularly important, when comparing this view with that of the monetarists, to note that there is no necessity for such increase in

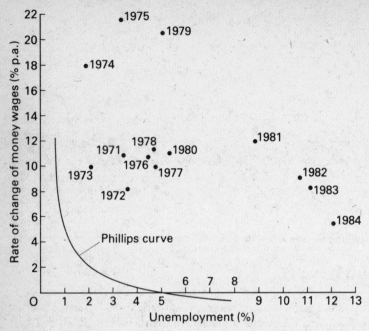

Fig. 8.2 The Phillips curve

expenditure to be accompanied by an increase in money supply. An increase in the money supply, if it lowers interest rates, *may* encourage more investment for example, but aggregate demand can increase *independently of* any change in the money supply.

The Phillips curve made another contribution to the Keynesian interpretation of inflation. It suggested the possible relevance of prices and incomes policies. One line of argument started with the assumption that the government, and the community, would always seek the lowest possible level of unemployment. The Phillips curve message, however, was that this was likely to cause conflict with the aim of price stability. But, if people could be persuaded to hold down their costs in circumstances where they might be tempted to raise them, then the community could enjoy a lower rate of inflation with any given level of unemployment. In the jargon of the day, a prices and incomes policy could improve the inflation/unemployment trade-off by 'displacing the Phillips curve to the left'.

Another argument which also led to the prices and incomes policy conclusion lay in the shape of the Phillips curve. Although it was roughly L-shaped, it took the form of a smooth curve. That is to say, there was no level of unemployment at which demand suddenly became excessive and inflation suddenly took off. This led some economists to the conclusion that the gentle take-off into inflation must be caused by some trade unions, raw material suppliers and so on taking advantage of the relatively high level of demand to increase their prices. Again, if they could be persuaded not to do this, then the economy could be run at lower unemployment/inflation combination.

The outstanding difficulty with this explanation as it stands, of course, is its apparent inability to cope with events in the 1970s and 1980s. We have added to Fig. 8.2 the pairs of wage/unemployment data for 1971 to 1984 and these can all be seen to lie dramatically to the right of the original curve. If this were all, one might be tempted to say 'the curve has shifted'. This would mean that the inverse relationship still held (and therefore the Keynesian view is still possibly correct) but that something had happened to raise the recorded level of unemployment at which 'full employment' occurs. Unfortunately, the scatter of the data prevents any fitting of a single new curve. The best that can be said is that the data for the 1970s possibly hint at an inverse relationship on a new curve (though the fit is very poor) and that the data for the 1980s suggest yet a third possible curve.

8.2.2 The monetarist explanation

Like the original Keynesian view, the monetarist explanation of inflation suggests that it is the result of attempts by the community to spend more on goods and services than the economy can currently produce. There are two differences, however.

Firstly, the origin of the excess spending is very specifically identified by the monetarists: it lies in the rate of growth of the money stock. If the money stock grows more rapidly than the economy's ability to produce, then inflation will inevitably follow. Equally, it is asserted, inflation cannot occur without the excessive monetary growth. In more formal language, excess monetary growth is identified as both a sufficient and a necessary condition for inflation.

Secondly, monetarists have a different interpretation of what it is that limits the economy's ability to produce. We saw above that Keynesians have always recognised that excess demand at full employment would be inflationary. 'Full employment' was thought of as being represented by some absolute figure for recorded unemployment and it was also thought that the economy might at any particular time be 'in equilibrium' at something other than full employment. Therefore it was possible for governments to vary the level of aggregate demand and thus to choose the level of output and employment. Further, given the Phillips curve information, they could choose the level of output and employment in the light of the rate of inflation they were prepared to accept. In contrast, monetarists would say that the level of output and employment (and therefore unemployment) is given, and cannot be affected by varying the level of aggregate demand. The economy always tends to a position of labour market-clearing, that is to say, the economy is always at 'full employment'.

Once again, as in Chapter 7, we are being given an analysis of each side of the quantity theory equation. Remember the equation:

$$M \times V = P \times T$$

On the left-hand side (as we said in sect. 7.3) there is a view about the nature of people's demand for money balances that means that changes in those balances (that is, in the supply of money), will be reflected in changes in spending. Velocity is assumed to be stable, changing little over time. It is therefore changes in M which lead to changes in aggregate demand.

On the right-hand side (as we said in sect. 7.4) there is a view of the labour market which says that the market always clears. Thus we have 'full employment' although this may leave us with, in practice, any level of recorded unemployment – the 'natural rate of unemployment'.

Most important, for our present analysis, was our tracing out in section 7.4 of the sequence of events that would follow if an increase in aggregate demand occurred when the labour market was in equilibrium. Remember, firms would try to increase output in response (and might temporarily succeed) but costs would rise, pushing them back to the original level of output, but of course with higher prices. To complete our understanding of the monetarists' claim that it is the rate of growth of the money supply that is crucial, we need only add to our analysis in Chapter 7, that productivity will tend to rise over time and that (even with a given level of 'full' employment) output will tend to increase. In the above equation T now has a built-in rate of growth. Thus, if this growing volume of transactions, T, is to be financed, the money supply has to grow by just enough to keep pace. If it exceeds this 'natural' rate of growth of the economy, there will be too much spending and prices will rise.

To complete this summary picture of the monetarist theory of inflation it is worth looking at what it says about the Phillips curve. After all, it was the Phillips curve's inability to cope with recent evidence that gave an impetus to the search for an alternative explanation of inflation.

The policy implication of the Phillips curve was that governments could choose between unemployment and inflation. Any level of unemployment is feasible provided one is prepared to accept the inflationary consequences. If, however, the economy always tends to a market clearing level of employment (and therefore to a 'natural' rate of unemployment this cannot be true. In any diagram with unemployment on the horizontal axis, the 'natural' level will be shown by a vertical line, as in Fig. 8.3.

If governments are unhappy with such a level of unemployment they may attempt to reduce it by stimulating aggregate demand and they may temporarily have some success. Suppose, looking at Fig. 8.3, that we start with unemployment at 'A' and zero wage inflation. An expansion in demand may take us to 'B': as firms try to increase output, they hire more labour and have to offer a higher money wage to persuade more people to work. Since we previously had zero money wage inflation, this higher money wage is interpreted as a rise in real wages. Temporarily at least, we have lower unemployment but higher (i.e. now positive) wage inflation. This

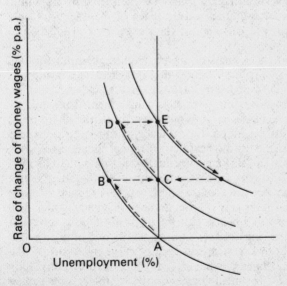

Fig 8.3 The vertical Phillips curve

is exactly the sequence we described in section 7.4.2. What we also said there, however, was that because all markets were initially in equilibrium, all prices would rise and people, workers and firms alike, would realise that there had been no change in real rewards, so that their behaviour would revert to the original quantities. In Fig. 8.3, therefore, unemployment will revert to 'A'. Unfortunately, what has changed is people's expectations about prices. The maintenance of constant real values is now associated with a positive rate of wage and price inflation. If workers are not to revise their behaviour again, they will need to know that their real wage is safe; that is, that money wages will go on rising at the established rate of price inflation. Transactors now 'expect' a given rate of inflation. In Fig. 8.3 we are at position 'C'.

If governments are unconvinced by their failure to produce a lasting reduction in the level of unemployment, and repeat the demand stimulus, then the same process will recur. This time, since we start from 'C' we shall go initially to 'D' and then revert to 'E'. In the long run, there is no avoiding the 'natural' rate of unemployment which will always be at 'A', though it is true that governments can 'choose' to have this level of unemployment with any rate of inflation. The choice of options in Fig. 8.3 is 'A' or 'C' or 'E'. This is equivalent to saying that in the long run the Phillips curve is vertical though it may be intersected by an infinite number of short-term Phillips curves. Each of these lasts for only as long as it takes people to adjust their expections of inflation to the rate now ruling.

Equally important is what the theory implies about attempts to reduce the rate of inflation. A reduction in aggregate demand (via a reduction in the growth rate of the money stock) can have no more lasting effect upon the level of unemployment than could an increase in aggregate demand. What happens in the short term, however, depends again on how quickly people's expectations adjust. If adjustments to the new, lower, rate of inflation are slow, and people persist in striking bargains based upon the old rate, they will find the money stock inadequate to finance the volume of transactions at that price level. There will be a reduction in the volume of transactions and a rise in unemployment which will persist until transactors realise that they have to trade at lower (or more slowly increasing) prices. During this period, the economy will have moved down a short-run Phillips curve (with lower inflation and higher unemployment) but once expectations have adjusted, the level of unemployment will fall to its long run or natural level. In section 8.4 we shall see that this need to get expectations to change rapidly if unemployment is to be avoided during a deflationary period lies behind the public announcement of target rates of inflation.

8.3 The costs of inflation

There are several *potential* costs one can list:

1. Inflation redistributes real income.
2. Inflation redistributes real wealth.
3. Inflation obstructs market signals.
4. Inflation makes exports less competitive/imports more competitive.
5. Inflation uses resources in keeping up with price changes.
6. Inflation involves more frequent trips to the bank.
7. Inflation causes unemployment.

How many of these cost occur *in practice* and how serious are they?

At the outset we have to make a distinction between 'anticipated' and 'unanticipated' inflation. Consider the case of real incomes. If inflation is 'fully anticipated' this means that people correctly foresee the rate of inflation and can take appropriate action – that is, can build it into their transactions. In the case of incomes this would mean that everyone's money income increased at exactly the same rate as inflation over a period of time. Plainly, in these circumstances there will be no effect on real income; everyone is in exactly the same position at the end of the period as they were in at the beginning. In contrast, if inflation is not fully anticipated so that some money incomes increased faster than others, then their recipients would enjoy a relative gain in real income.

1. Inflation and the redistribution of income

When we talk about redistribution we are talking about changes in the position of people relative to each other. Objections to such redistribution are twofold. Firstly, there is a popular suspicion that such redistribution in practice tends to work against people on low incomes, thus increasing poverty and inequality. Secondly, whether or not redistribution is systematically biased toward any particular group, it is arbitrary. That is to say that, unlike a deliberate policy of taxation to redistribute income, no democratic process has willed the redistribution that results from inflation.

To illustrate the redistribution from low to high income groups, it is common to focus on people with fixed money incomes and to take pensioners as a particular example. Unfortunately neither this, nor other examples, are very convincing if we wish to establish a general and systematic redistribution. Very few pensioners have a money income which is fixed. State benefits are explicitly linked to the level of money earnings generally in the economy and are therefore particularly well protected from a distributional point of view. Not all company pensions are formally linked to the general level of prices, but many now provide for periodic revision. The people who are really at risk are probably a rapidly decreasing number who qualified for an occupational pension many years ago when no revision was provided for. Some employees, particularly part-time and home-workers where union organisation is unusual, are also likely to suffer, and there have been times, during periods of incomes policy for example, when employees in the public sector have found their money incomes falling behind the general level and have had to wait for occasional reviews in order to catch up. What all of this shows is not that inflation never causes a redistribution of real income but that we have to look very carefully at the evidence in order to see who is affected and by how much. We cannot simply draw a sweeping picture with a broad brush by saying 'pensioners' or 'the low paid'.

2. Inflation and the redistribution of wealth

Similar conclusions emerge when we discuss real wealth. People can store their wealth in a variety of assets. Some of these are now formally 'index-linked', while others have proved to be so in practice because their nominal value has kept pace with inflation. In the UK there have been times when houses have risen in value by more than the rate of inflation. Some assets have a nominal value which is, however, fixed. Many financial assets are like this. Government bonds and building society deposits are good examples, and, of course, money is the extreme case. Thus the impact of inflation on one's wealth holdings depends upon the distribution of one's assets.

In practice, people who hold significant wealth do so in a variety of assets and there is little to suggest that many people hold a distinctively unfavourable portfolio (Piachaud 1978). This is what one would expect. As people have become used to living with inflation they have adjusted the form in which they save. Two groups of people are, however, worth mentioning because common sense suggests that they ought to be victims and beneficiaries respectively of the impact of inflation on real wealth.

Firstly, lenders ought to lose. This is because their assets (loans) are financial assets whose nominal value is fixed at the beginning of the period. At the end of the period they will be repaid the original sum but its real value will have fallen. In the mean time they will have received interest payments which can be regarded as compensation for this loss of capital value, but for long periods in the 1970s interest rates were below the rate of inflation. (This is what we mean by saying that 'real' interest rates were negative.)

Secondly, borrowers ought to gain. The borrower uses the loan to acquire a real asset which provides him with a service. Its nominal value (allowing for wear and tear) cannot do less than keep pace with inflation and may even exceed it. In the mean time he pays a rate of interest below the rate of inflation and repays a capital sum in a depreciated currency. This at least is the theory, and it points to the conclusion in particular that house purchasers with a mortgage should have gained at the expense of those who lend them money.

In practice, the picture is not so simple. Many borrowers are simultaneously lenders. Many homes buyers, for example, are building society depositors. What matters, therefore, is people's position as *net* borrowers and lenders and the specific terms on which they do their borrowing and lending. All that can be said from the few investigations that have been done (Piachaud 1978) is that there are no large, easily identifiable social groups who systematically win or lose. There may be (only may be) a tendency for real wealth in the 1970s to have been redistributed towards young married couples (with large mortgages and small savings) away from elderly people (with small mortgages and large savings). In the mid-1980s, this position looks like being reversed. Since 1980, inflation has fallen more rapidly than interest rates and since 1983 has been below the rate of interest paid on popular forms of savings such as building society deposits, National Savings and bank deposits. Real interest rates, in other words, have been positive and the transfer of real wealth has been towards net savers.

3. Inflation and market signals

Another problem with inflation, it is sometimes said, is that it makes market signals hard to interpret. This, predictably, is an argument against inflation used by those ('market optimists') who generally favour a market system of resource allocation. The argument is that when prices are rising, transactors find it hard to tell whether a particular price rise is a 'real' (or relative) price rise which requires a particular response from them or is simply the fact that their potential purchase is keeping pace with all other goods. For example, a firm on the point of installing a heating system, confronted by a big increase in the price of oil, may take this to mean that oil is now more expensive *relative to* other fuels and may install alternative, say gas-fired, equipment which under the previous cost conditions was less suitable. Now suppose that after installation the price of gas and other fuels catches up with that of oil. Thus the increase in the cost of oil was not a relative increase at all but merely reflected the fact that in inflation prices may go up at a similar rate over time, but that they do not all do so on the same day. With the old price relativities established, our firm may find that it has made the wrong decision.

Once again, the situation is easy to imagine in principle but does it happen in practice? If all depends on whether transactors know the current rate of inflation. In our example, all the firm had to do was to subtract from the oil price increase the established rate of inflation. In theory, it would then have been left with the same infromation that it would have had under price stability. It seems reasonable, after fifteen years of inflation, to suppose that people know that inflation exists, that they know the established rate and that they do the appropriate calculations. A problem arises, however, where the rate of inflation is not stable. In these circumstances the established (i.e. known) rate of inflation may not be the same as the current rate. In such circumstances, subtracting the known rate may not give us a good guide to the present situation. Or again the time lags in the response of different commodities to inflation may not be stable. In our example it may be true last year that gas and electricity prices followed the rise in oil prices, but this year the equivalent response may be delayed, or may not take place at all.

Note that we are now saying that it is instability, or volatility, of inflation that is the problem. This is not the same as 'high' or 'low' inflation. It has at times been assumed that high rates of inflation do in fact go hand in hand with greater variability but the evidence for this is far from conclusive (Bootle 1981).

4. Inflation and external trade

If one country has a rate of inflation which is significantly greater than that of its trading partners its exports will tend to become dearer and its imports cheaper. On the assumption of reasonable demand elasticities, the balance of payments will deteriorate, causing eventual problems of external finance and a reduction in domestic real income. The extent to which all this happens depends upon the exchange rate regime in force. With fixed exchange rates, these consequences will follow fairly directly. This is because under such a regime, overseas buyers have to surrender a constant number of francs, for example, for a given number of pounds. Inflation means that UK goods cost more in pounds, so that more francs must also be given up in order to buy them, thereby discouraging the purchase of exports. In contrast, French imports into the UK are cheaper.

In a regime of floating exchange rates a country with a high rate of inflation will find that its currency depreciates in value against the currencies of its trading partners. Thus, although the price of goods in pounds may have gone up, since pounds are cheaper to buy with francs the price to French customers may not have increased. In a world of freely floating rates and perfect foreign exchange markets, the purchasing power parity theory suggests that movements in the external value of a currency should exactly offset any differential in internal rates of inflation.

In practice, exchange rates do not adjust freely and therefore a country with a differential rate of inflation is likely to experience some quantity changes in its external trade as well as in domestic output and employment. Since 1972, for example, the pound has fluctuated anything but freely against other currencies (although over the period the trend has been decidely downwards) and British exports have been encouraged when the pound has fallen and discouraged when the pound has risen.

A number of reasons lie behind exchange rate frictions. Firstly, exchange rates are influenced by capital flows as well as by payment for goods and services. In the UK, for example, a policy of tight monetary control since 1979 has been responsible for higher interest rates than those prevailing in some other financial centres. This has meant that UK financial assets have been relatively attractive and purchases of sterling in order to buy these assets has kept the exchange rate above what would probably be justified on the grounds of comparative production costs.

Secondly, governments may deliberately intervene in foreign exchange markets in order to prevent adjustments even though nominally following a floating rate regime. Sometimes this is done to 'smooth' the rate, preventing an adjustment which is thought to be only temporary. Sometimes it is done when governments are sensitive to movements in some general price index. One of the effects of depreciation, after all, is to raise the price of imports, and therefore inflation, so that the UK government (as in the spring of 1985) has sometimes intervened to buy the pound.

So far, the costs we have looked at rely heavily upon people failing to anticipate inflation correctly. Two costs which are sometimes said to apply even where anticipation is correct are numbers five and six in our list.

5 and 6. Inflation: the 'menu' and 'shoe leather' costs

If inflation is correctly foreseen and therefore causes no other distortions it will require resources to be used in frequently changing prices. This is sometimes referred to as the 'menu cost', the cost of frequently updating the prices on a restaurant menu. As Bootle says, 'making the decisions, changing the price tags, slot machines, wage arrangements disseminating the information, all take time, effort and money' (Bootle 1981: 37).

Rather similarly, at high rates of inflation there are a number of incentives to economies on holding cash balances (which do not bear interest) even though with higher prices there is a need for more cash. At the trivial (Friedman 1969) level, this imposes a 'shoe leather cost' as people have to make more frequent trips to the bank. Conceivably, the incentives to economise on holding cash balances could become so great as to interfere with trade. This was the case in Germany in 1923 where money became unacceptable and cigarettes and sometimes even barter were substituted. But the German experience was quite unique and unrepresentative of what we normally have in mind when we worry about inflation.

At no rate of inflation remotely worth considering do either of these costs look very significant.

7. Inflation and unemployment

In recent years government ministers have argued that inflation causes unemployment. It should be noted that this is a reversal of the Phillips curve relationship discussed above in section 8.2.1. If this were true, it would indeed be a powerful argument for taking a strong anti-inflation stance. There are four possible ways in which one could develop a case that inflation reduces employment and output.

The first argument is that inflation causes unemployment because when finally a deflationary policy is introduced this reduces demand and raises unemployment. This is absurd because it assumes what it sets out to prove. Unless one has already decided that inflation is evil why should one want to institute a policy which has 'bad' consequences?

The second and third arguments rely upon inflation causing shifts, respectively, in the distribution of real income and real wealth. If inflation were to raise real wages at the expense of real profits this would depress investment and output. Rather similarly, if inflation erodes the real value of savings, and people respond by reducing consumption in order to rebuild their savings, then again expenditure and demand will fall. But we have already established that significant redistributional effects are hard to find. It is true that the profit share in national income fell rapidly in 1980 (to about 10 per cent by the last quarter) but this coincided with a falling rate of inflation and with a deflationary policy which acted, as all do initially, upon the firms' prices. Again, if it is true that inflation 'causes' unemployment because it reduces real demand in the economy, it is perverse to argue that we must have deflation of demand in the economy in order to reduce inflation.

Fourthly, it is possible to argue that inflation causes uncertainty, thereby reducing investment spending. Once again, this is the argument about volatility. Firms will be deterred from investment projects if they think that current rates of inflation are not an accurate reflection of the way in which prices will move in future. Given a steady rate of inflation, however, how is 10 per cent more 'uncertain' than 1 per cent? Only if it is the case that the volatility of inflation increases at higher rates of inflation, should uncertainty be associated with inflation. We said earlier the evidence was 'fragile'.

On the evidence, the most convincing conclusion one can draw about the inflation-unemployment relation is not that it is positive at all, but that it is inverse. After five years of deflation the government has been successful in reducing inflation to less than 5 per cent. In the same period, unemployment has risen to record levels and at a record rate. This is exactly what one would expect from a Keynes–Phillips prediction. Of course, one may argue that deflation has only pushed the economy down a short-run Phillips curve and when (in the long run!) people's expectations of inflation have adjusted downwards, unemployment will fall to its natural rate. It is of more than passing interest that no government spokesmen can now be heard to predict a fall in the level of unemployment in spite of the historically low rate of inflation. This is hardly a sign of government conviction that inflation really does cause unemployment.

8.4 The medium-term financial strategy

Whatever one may think of the wisdom of current policy, one is obliged to understand it. The conduct of policy is based fairly directly upon views about the way in which the economy works which we have examined in other chapters. What follows is an outline of the policy and in parentheses we have shown the sections in which the foundations are discussed.

Given the view that inflation is the most important of the UK's economic problems, it is not surprising that the first, and perhaps overriding feature, of the 'medium-term financial strategy' (MTFS) is the belief that governments can and should control the rate of monetary growth. The rationale for this is that changes in aggregate spending can occur only if there are changes in the supply of money (sect. 7.3), and that the economy's ability to respond to changes in spending through changes in output rather than prices is determined by its 'natural' rate of growth (sect. 8.2.2). The ultimate aim is therefore to supply an increase in the money stock which just matches the long-term rate of growth of output at current prices. Unfortunately, since excess monetary growth and inflation were both established features of the economy when the policy was introduced, the achievement of this aim must begin with successive reductions in the rate of monetary growth. Target rates of growth and the outturns are given in Table 8.2.

It is clear that whatever the rationale behind monetary targets they have not been easy to achieve. In practice, this has been due

Table 8.2 Growth of £M_3

Date	Target (% p.a.)	Out-turn (% p.a.)
1976/7	9–13	7.7
1977/8	9–13	16.0
1978/9	8–12	10.9
1979/80	7–11	17.8
1980/1	7–11	18.5
1981/2	6–10	14.5
1982/3	8–12	9.8
1983/4	7–11	11.6
1984/5	6–10	9.6
1985/6	5–9	14.8

Source: Bank of England Quarterly Bulletin,
respective Mar. issues

to difficulties in estimating the strength of private sector demand for bank lending.

This concern with monetary growth is partly responsible for the second feature of the MTFS, namely the concern with the public sector borrowing requirement (PSBR). This arises because it can be shown (sect. 6.3) that there is a *possible* relationship between the size of the PSBR and increases in the money supply. There has therefore been concern to reduce the PSBR by reducing public expenditure because this, it is argued, is the only satisfactory way of avoiding the unwanted additions to the money stock. This conclusion is arrived at by rejecting an increase in taxation as a way of reducing the PSBR because of the effect upon incentives (sect. 2.2). The other possibility, namely accepting a given PSBR and financing it by selling sufficient government debt to avoid the monetary expansion, it also rejected because of the supposed impact on interest rates (sect. 6.4). Note in passing how this feature of the MTFS is consistent with other aspects of government policy (see ch. 3) aimed at promoting the private rather than the public sectors.

The third and final feature of the MTFS which is worth noting is its emphasis upon rates of change for these variables expressed for some years ahead.

The MTFS provides at least two sources of contrast with what we called Keynesian stabilisation policy (ch. 5).

Firstly because we are concerned here with the price level rather than with output and employment, we are concerned with planning *financial* rather than *real* magnitudes. Secondly, the nature of such planning involves the government surrendering its ability to make short-term responses to changes in the economy: i.e. it involves the substitution of 'rules' for 'discretion'. The arguments behind this are many but we have touched on two.

The first is that the short-term planning and manipulation of the economy through tax rates and public spending are so difficult that governments' attempts have in practice tended to increase rather than diminish instability (sect. 5.6).

The second is that to make the right decisions transactors need 'good' information. Governments can help in this respect by avoiding frequent changes in economic variables and, better still, by announcing the values of those variables for as far ahead as possible (sect. 5.6). Also, announcing, and keeping to, rates of monetary growth for the future helps people to 'revise' their expectations appropriately. This is important since reducing inflation with as little disruption as possible to employment and output involves changing people's expectations about inflation (sect. (8.2.2). If individuals and firms go on increasing their contract prices when monetary growth is falling, then there will be bankruptcies and unemployment. The MTFS can in this sense be seen as an aid to providing transactors with appropriate information for the future.

Further reading

Still one of the best introductions to theories of inflation is Trevithick (1980). The final chapter on the policy recommendations following from each theory is also useful. Also very good on theories, costs, policy and evidence is Griffiths and Wall (1984) Ch. 8.

Two articles which examine the evidence for the costs of inflation (and generally find it unconvincing) are by Bootle (1981) and Higham and Tomlinson (1982).

One theory of inflation, the cost-push or institutionalist theory, we have not dealt with here because of its outright rejection by government in recent years. An entertaining and thoroughly readable account is in Galbraith (1975) Ch. 18.

Monthly data on movements in retail prices are published in the *Employment Gazette* in considerable detail. The *Gazette* also has occasional articles on the construction and interpretation of the retail price index. More summary information on price movements appear in *Economic Trends*. Detailed information on the behaviour of money supply and public sector borrowing is in *Financial Statistics* (monthly) and the *Bank of England Quarterly Bulletin*. The latter is particularly useful since it includes commentary on policy and background information on targets and objectives. Again, more summary information is published in *Economic Trends*.

Questions

*: Answers to these questions are discussed in Part II.

1. Summarise and evaluate monetarist recommendations for macroeconomic policy. (Oxford, June 1980)

2.* 'Inflation is the single most important economic problem.' Discuss. (London, June 1981)

3.* Explain the relationships which may exist between inflation and unemployment. (ACA, June 1983)

4.★ Evaluate the arguments for and against rigid adherence to a pre-announced rate of growth of a single monetary aggregate. (Oxford, June 1982)

5. 'Inflation is entirely a monetary phenomenon that can only be overcome by effective control of the money supply.' Discuss. (AEB, June 1984)

Part two

Specimen answers

Chapter 1

1. (a) Explain the 'mixed economy' approach to the allocation of scarce resources.
    (b) What factors determine the extent to which an economy is mixed? (ACA, June 1982)

The term 'the mixed economy' refers to economic systems which allocate scarce resources through a combination of the public and private sectors. The 'mixed economy' approach starts from the view that under ideal circumstances the private market economy would provide the most efficient way of allocating resources. The assumptions necessary to support this view are set out in section 1.2.1 on pp. 11 and 12 and may be summed up by the phrase *perfect competition*. However, it is accepted that many of these conditions do not apply in practice and that, for a variety of reasons, there may be *market failure* in real economies. The possibility of market failure then provides a justification for government intervention in the market economy.

We summarise the arguments for government intervention under six headings from pp. 12 to 18. In particular, a market economy left to itself would face difficulties in the provision of *public goods* because people (free riders) would be able to consume these goods without having paid for them. Several examples are provided in the text. A further major problem for the market lies in the existence of social or external costs and benefits. It is these which enter into arguments for government intervention in the fields of health, education, pollution control and so on. Other important arguments for government intervention include the existence of monopolies and the lack of information in markets. It is the notion that people either lack information or are not always the best judge of their own welfare that leads to some goods being regarded as merit or demerit goods. Governments are given the roles of encouraging the consumption of merit goods and of discouraging or preventing the consumption of demerit goods. Finally, government intervention is seen as necessary by supporters of the 'mixed economy' approach to produce a more equitable distribution of income and wealth than that which would result from an unfettered market economy.

We can see that the extent to which an economy is mixed will depend on the importance of each of these cases. To some extent we can see that changes in the nature of a society will change the importance of some cases. Thus, as populations have grown and become more urbanised there has been a great increase in the degree of *interdependence* within them. This means that the actions of individuals have a greater impact on other people than before. In other words, there has been a great increase in the size of external costs and benefits. Interdependence has increased for a variety of other reasons also, including changes in the nature of production processes (greater specialisation). Again, one could argue that as society has become more complex and the quantity of human knowledge has expanded, it has become more difficult for people to have the knowledge necessary for them to make the best possible decision. Many other such arguments have been put forward to account for the movement away from the private sector to the public sector which has taken place in all Western mixed economies over the past one hundred years.

However, we have also seen that widely differing opinions can be held as to how well markets work. We have distinguished between market optimists and market pessimists. *Market optimists* clearly favour a small role for the public sector within the mixed economy. Thus, there can be no definite answer as to how the division between the two sectors should be made. It will be different at different times and will also be different among societies which in other ways have many things in common, such as those of the UK and the US.

2. Explain, with examples, the terms 'external costs' and 'external benefits'. Why and how might the government discourage activities involving excessive external costs? (London, Jan. 1984).

We discuss external costs and benefits under the heading of 'social costs and benefits' on pp. 13 and 14. They are costs and benefits associated with the provision of goods and services in an economy which fall on people other than those directly involved in the production and consumption of the commodities. We can say that in a free market producers, when deciding what they are going to produce and how they are going to produce it, will take into account only those costs which they must pay and which will affect the profit they make (that is, the *private* costs of acquiring factors of production and combining them in an act of production). Equally, a consumer will decide how much he or she is willing to pay for a commodity on the basis of the satisfaction he or she will obtain personally from it. However, the production and consumption of a commodity may affect other people – people who are not in a position to influence the decisions of the producers and consumers.

We provide on p. 13 an example of an external benefit arising from education. On p. 47 we point out that investment in the economy's infrastructure (for instance on transport, fuel and telecommunications) may have considerable external benefits through its influence on the international competitiveness of British firms. Other examples related to nationalised industries are provided in section 3.5.2 and on p. 46 we introduce the special example of a *caring externality* where a society is held to benefit generally from the knowledge that it is looking after those in need.

Examples of external costs include the cases of smoking chimneys and inadequately tested drugs (p. 14) and the costs arising from growth in the size of lorries and the motorway network (p. 54). The easiest examples of external costs to discuss are those which relate to pollution and the environment. A controversial one in recent years has concerned possible external costs associated with the dumping of nuclear waste; in particular worries about the impact of the activities of British Nuclear Fuels on Cumbrian beaches and the Cumbrian tourist industry and on the Isle of Man's fishing industry.

If we accept the view that a nation's scarce resources should be used to maximise the well-being of society as a whole, it follows that decisions as to the use of resources should take into account total costs and benefits, not just those which private markets can deal with (or *internalise*). We can easily see from the diagram below that the failure to consider external costs may lead to a good being over-provided.

Here the supply curve S_1S_1 is the supply curve of the industry producing the good and includes only private costs. Including external costs would push the supply curve up to S_2S_2 and would reduce equilibrium output to OQ_2. Government might intervene to ensure this outcome in a number of ways. It could impose a tax

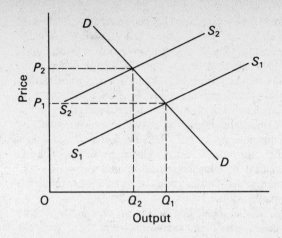

on the industry equal to the estimated external costs. This would push up the supply curve as shown in the diagram. Alternatively, it could introduce regulations governing the production of the industry to force the industry to take account of external costs. For example, regulations might limit the places where industrial waste can be dumped or might require additional treatment of the waste before it is dumped. Or, industries may be required to obtain planning permission before some types of production can be undertaken in particular areas. A more extreme form of government intervention in the market would be for government to take over fully responsibility for the industry. Then, government decisions would replace market decisions. Where this happens for a whole economy we have a *planned economy*.

There are two provisos which should be made to the argument that excessive external costs justify government intervention in the market. The first is that it cannot be assumed that governments themselves always take into account the full social costs of their actions (see p. 14). The second is that under some circumstances markets may be able to internalise external costs and benefits if property rights are more clearly defined (see p. 14).

5. What are the main differences between public and private goods? What factors should determine the charges made for school meals? (Oxford, June 1979)

There are two important differences between public and private goods. The first is that people cannot be excluded from consumption of a public good. Thus, those who do not pay may benefit from the provision of public goods (the problem of the *free rider*, which is discussed on pp. 12 and 13). Equally, once a public good is provided it cannot be rejected. Private goods, on the other hand, can be enjoyed solely by the owner of the good. The second difference is that public goods are non-rival or non-competitive in consumption. This means that they are not diminished by being consumed by one person and remain available to be consumed by others. In our discussion on p. 12, we use here the standard example of the light from a lighthouse. An important implication is that the marginal cost of allowing an additional person to consume the good is zero. Pure public goods are both non-excludable and non-rival in consumption.

By this definition, school meals are clearly private goods – those who do not pay could easily be excluded from them and the provision of a meal for an additional child involves some additional or marginal cost. Therefore we could argue that school meals should be provided by an unfettered market. In this case, the rules regarding the best use of resources would require that the price of a school meal should be equal to its marginal cost. We consider the marginal cost pricing argument in section 3.5.1. Marginal cost pricing will ensue with profit maximising firms under conditions of perfect competition. Given the size of schools, however, the idea of large numbers of small sellers providing meals in a school is absurd. It would not be a good use of resources to have different small sellers in each school, because the provision of meals certainly involves economies of scale (see sect. 4.3.2). One could imagine firms providing meals to a number of schools but local monopolies would certainly develop in a free market. The seller in a particular school would face a downward sloping demand curve and price would not equal marginal cost. The result would be (as shown in sect. 3.5.1) that the output of school meals would be too low and the price too high. Thus, a subsidy may be justified in order to produce the perfectly competitive outcome.

A quite different argument for a subsidy for school meals can be derived from the view that the provision of school meals carries with it an external benefit. We could claim, for example, that children who do not eat enough at lunchtime perform badly in their schoolwork and do not make full use of their abilities. This is a loss for society as a whole since human abilities are a scarce resource. We could represent this case with the diagram below.

D_1D_1 is the demand curve of school children for school meals.

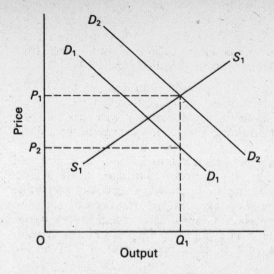

However, if the external benefits were considered, the demand curve would be D_2D_2. From a social viewpoint the output should be OQ_1. To ensure that OQ_1 is consumed, a price of only OP_2 will need to be charged. P_2P_1 will then indicate the subsidy to be paid on each meal. Instead of just considering the quantity of food provided, we could say that even if children had adequate money to spend on school meals, they may lack knowledge as to which foods are good for them and may spend unwisely. Then we could introduce the idea of merit goods and say that particular kinds of school meals (those meeting some established nutritional standard) should be subsidised. (For a consideration of merit goods see p. 15).

Finally, we could introduce the question of income distribution. It may be that society is concerned that poor children are being inadequately fed. This could simply justify an argument for income redistribution among families so that poor parents could, if they so chose, give their children more money for school meals. However, society may not be worried about poverty in general but may be disturbed specifically by the idea of malnourished children. If this were the case, we might argue for the provision of goods in kind (that is, the provision of free or heavily subsidised school meals to poor children) rather than the transfer of money income to poor families. This is the idea that is dealt with in the section on caring externalities on p. 46.

Chapter 2

1. Discuss the case for shifting the balance of taxation away from direct taxes to indirect taxes. (London, June 1984)

We have considered this argument from pp. 30 to 37. We concluded our discussion there by suggesting that there was no convincing case in favour of indirect taxes overall but that there may be a case for maintaining some sort of balance between direct and indirect taxes.

The arguments most often used in favour of indirect taxes do not seem strong. Thus the view that they allow more choice is fallacious since if indirect taxes are to provide a significant proportion of tax revenue they must be such that they cannot easily be avoided. Anyway, we saw in Chapter 1 that changing one's behaviour to avoid a tax involves a cost in the form of an excess burden. We considered this on p. 8, using the example of VAT on hot take-away foods.

The notion that direct taxes penalise savers we also saw to relate to the particular form of some direct taxes rather than to direct taxes as a whole. Thus, if the present tax system is thought to discourage savers and perhaps, therefore, to affect investment in the economy, the problem could be tackled by reforming the existing direct taxes. It is not necessary to switch to indirect taxes. Arguments concerning effects on incentives and on administration and compliance costs are not particularly in favour of indirect taxes. The only clear point in favour of indirect taxes is that they may assist a country's trading position since taxes paid on exported goods are refundable (see p. 36). Against this one can set the possibility that indirect taxes are more inflationary than direct taxes. On balance, indirect taxes as usually operated are also regressive (that is, the taxes paid by richer people make up a *smaller* proportion of their incomes than is true for poorer people). However, whether this is regarded as good or bad depends entirely on one's objectives.

All of this leaves us only with the question of balance between the two kinds of taxes. The argument here derives from the general proposition that if a single type of tax is used to generate a large proportion of total tax revenue, marginal rates of that tax may need to be very high. Since it is marginal tax rates which are held to provide disincentives in the economy, a case can be made for using several tax bases and raising total taxation revenues in a variety of ways. We suggest on p. 37 that economic theory provides no definite guidance as to the nature of balance among different kinds of tax. In the 1970s, however, failure to adjust indirect tax rates in line with inflation did lead to revenue from indirect taxes falling considerably as a proportion of total tax revenue. Thus there was a case for reversing this trend and returning to the proportions which had existed previously. In addition, the raising of VAT to 15 per cent in 1979 considerably reduced average administration costs of VAT and, in doing so, may have reduced administration costs of the tax system as a whole. Whether or not there should be a continued move towards indirect taxes is a different matter. In practice, the attitudes of different groups towards the two types of tax appear to be bound closely to their attitudes towards the desirability of income redistribution from poor to rich.

2. Discuss the effects that an increase in social security payments might have on the level of unemployment. (London, June 1979).

The theoretical possibility that social security payments might have an effect on the level of unemployment can be shown using a simple modification of Fig. 2.1 (see p. 26).

   All we have done is to add to the diagram a vertical line indicating the worker's non-wage income. In this case we can treat this as the social security payments available to an unemployed worker, assuming that an employed worker receives no such payments. We

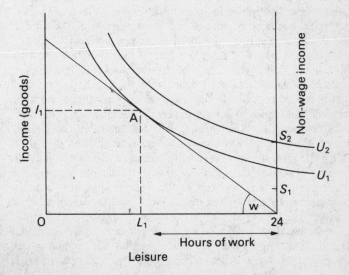

can then see that a worker who could obtain S_1 social security payments through not working, will choose to work, choosing OL_1 hours of leisure and working the rest of the day. This, remember, is because at the existing wage rate the worker maximises utility at point A. Now suppose that the social security payments to the unemployed are raised to S_2. It is clear that the worker will be better off (that is, on the higher indifference curve U_2) by choosing not to work. Hence an incease in social security payments may lead some workers to choose to become unemployed rather than work. In practice things are a good deal more complicated since some social security benefits may be available to workers whether they are in or out of work (child benefit, for instance) and workers are able to earn some income before they are taxed. Further, some social security payments are means-tested (that is, scaled according to the recipient's income from other sources). In reality, too, the decision of a worker is likely to be influenced by the incomes and work decisions of the rest of the household. None the less, the above diagram illustrates the general principle that social security payments may influence work decisions.

It is important to note that this form of analysis assumes that unemployment is voluntary (that is, that the unemployed are in a general sense choosing unemployment). This is the view of supply-side economics which we have considered in section 7.4.3. Keynesians argue that unemployment essentially arises from lack of demand in the economy and thus reject the form of analysis we have used above. Supply-side economists explain the relationship between social security payments and unemployment in a variety of ways. For example, it is held that the existence of social security payments leads workers to have less fear of unemployment and to demand higher wages than they otherwise would. These higher wages are then thought to price more workers out of the market. Again, it is argued that because of social security payments workers who become unemployed spend longer in looking for jobs they would like to have. In other words, they become more choosy. If, on average, the unemployed spend a longer time without jobs than used to be the case, the level of unemployment measured at a point in time will be higher than before. Whatever the particular form of the argument, much depends on the relationship between the income a person receives when out of work and the income he or she receives when in work. This relationship has become known as the *replacement ratio* and many attempts have been made to measure it. The supply-side argument is that the higher social security payments are and hence the higher the replacement ratio is, the higher unemployment will be. As with other questions concerning incentives, theory provides no clear answer. Empirical research to date has generally suggested that the level of social security payments contributes only a little to the level of unemployment though the issue is still a controversial one.

3. Discuss the main objectives of taxation, illustrating your answer with reference to the UK's system of taxation. (AEB, June 1985)

Society needs taxation in order to pay for goods and services which it requires government to provide. Although governments can borrow and in most years in recent times in most western countries have spent more than they have collected in taxation (that is, run budget deficits), most government expenditure has to be met from taxation. Thus the main objective of taxation can be said to be the raising of revenue. It is usual, therefore, to argue that indirect taxes should be imposed on goods which have an inelastic demand so that the increase in the price of the goods resulting from the tax will cause only a small reduction in the demand for the good. In the UK, this is one of the principal arguments for the high excise taxes on alcohol and tobacco. Indeed, it is sometimes claimed that the government does not wish to strive too hard to discourage young people from smoking and drinking for fear of losing large amounts of taxation revenue! Again, a tax which is not actually paid by many people raises little revenue. When the top rate of income tax in the UK was lowered from 83 per cent to 60 per cent by the Thatcher government total tax revenue fell only slightly as a result because the 83 per cent rate had applied to very few taxpayers. The reform of the UK corporation tax system announced in the 1984 budget also partly stemmed from the fact that under the previously existing rules a number of companies were paying no tax at all.

Given that a government has decided to raise a certain amount of revenue through taxation, we can then distinguish three objectives in the design of a tax system. We have listed these in section 2.3 in terms of the impact of different taxes on resource allocation, income distribution and the costs of collection of taxation. We have considered a number of aspects of each of these in Chapters 1 and 2.

Thus, with regard to resource allocation, we looked in section 1.1.2 at the idea of excess burden – the notion that taxes interfere with freedom of choice by leading people to behave differently.

From the point of view of a country's GNP, the most important issue of this type is the effect of taxation on the labour supply. This is dealt with in detail in section 2.2. The principal argument for UK tax changes in recent years (including the reduction in the top rate of income tax, the reduction of the base rate of income tax from 33 to 29 per cent and the raising of the income threshold at which people start paying tax) has been that they will increase incentives to work.

In relation to the distribution of income, we have considered the questions of vertical and horizontal equity (see Sect. 2.1.2). There have been many debates relevant to these questions in recent years. These include criticism of the regressive nature of national insurance contributions, argument over tax relief on mortgage interest payments (which is of relevance to both vertical and horizontal equity) and the claim that the current UK tax system discriminates unfairly against women.

Under the heading of collection costs, one should include compliance costs (see sect. 1.1.2). For this reason, a tax system should, if possible, be simple and easy to understand. At the same time the system should be such that it is difficult for people to avoid (legally or illegally) paying taxes. The problem is that these two objectives almost inevitably conflict. Tax accountants and lawyers spend large amounts of time finding ways around tax legislation. In attempting to overcome this, the government introduces more legislation, people seek new loopholes and so the process goes on. One argument for lower tax rates is that they will provide people with less incentive to attempt to reduce their tax bills.

We can see, in summary, that there are two overwhelming difficulties in designing tax systems. Firstly, the tax system to be designed must take account of the amount of revenue the government wishes to raise and this is interrelated with questions such as the desirable level of government expenditure and the cost of government borrowing. Secondly, there seem bound to be conflicts among major objectives of a tax system, most notably between resource allocation (efficiency) and income distribution (equity).

Chapter 3

1. To what extent can the efficiency of a nationalised industry be judged from the size of its financial surplus or deficit? (London, June 1983)

This question is answered in detail in section 3.5. There we suggest that although the efficiency of a nationalised industry may influence the financial surplus or deficit of the industry, we cannot judge its efficiency from its surplus or deficit. Thus, the financial position of a nationalised industry will be affected if there is managerial slack and low levels of labour productivity leading to production at cost levels well above the minimum.

However, the actual financial surplus or deficit may also be influenced by the objectives set for the nationalised industry by government. For instance, in an attempt to improve resource allocation generally, government may require the industry to follow a marginal cost pricing rule. As we point out on p. 52, this policy in an industry characterised by declining long-run costs will produce a financial deficit. Again, government may require a nationalised industry to take account of social benefits and costs in its output and pricing policies. This too will have an impact on the industry's financial performance. The amount of borrowing which a nationalised industry is permitted may also have financial implications since it will influence the proportion of the industry's investment costs which has to be met from current revenue. In recent times, we have seen the government requiring several nationalised industries to produce increased surpluses in order to reduce the size of the public sector borrowing requirement for macroeconomic purposes. This may lead a nationalised industry to charge higher prices and produce at lower outputs than if it were attempting to meet consumer preferences and fulfil the requirements for allocative efficiency. In short, the reasons for an industry's financial performance may be many. Its efficiency will be only one of them.

2. Discuss the *economic* arguments for reducing the role of the state in the provision of health, education and housing in the UK. (AEB, June 1985)

People who argue for reducing the role of the state in the economy treat health, education and housing in much the same way as other commodities. Thus, their argument depends principally on the two general points outlined in section 3.3: that increased private production will introduce the profit motive and hence lead to a lowering of costs; and that competition will ensure that the type and quality of commodities which the consumer wants will be supplied. The lack of a profit motive in government provision leads, it is claimed, to bureaucratic procedures and waste. The direct supply of commodities without charge removes people's ability to influence the nature of the product through the market. Thus, health, education or housing or various elements of them may be over- or under-supplied. Decisions as to the nature of the product supplied are made by administrators and experts rather than by consumers. For example, it may be said that architects and planners were responsible for the explosion in the construction of high-rise housing in the 1960s, and that this was a type of housing which most people did not want. Or again that administrators and doctors have produced a more hospital-based and technology-centred health service than is in the best interests of most patients. Or, in education, that government provision has led to less stress being placed on educational basics (the 3 Rs) than most parents would like to see. Thus, more private provision would reduce what Friedman and others have referred to as the 'adverse externalities' of government intervention. These we list in section 3.3.3 as inefficiency, lack of choice and curtailment of freedom.

The case for maintaining government provision is set out in section 3.3.3 also. It is largely based on the existence of widespread external benefits in the provision of health, education and housing. A particular form of externality, *a caring externality*, is discussed in the section. This view puts much less weight on the importance of individual choice and much more on the needs of communities as a whole. Increased private provision, it is argued, would lead to competition to meet the needs of the well-off, since this is the area where profits can be made. The needs of the poor would not be met. Again, a *merit goods* argument as set out on p. 46 may be used. Finally, it is thought that health, education and housing are of such overwhelming social importance that their provision cannot be left to the market. Supporters of increased private provision play down the special nature of these areas of government provision.

3. Consider some of the reasons for any *one* nationalised industry making persistent financial losses, and discuss whether such losses should be eliminated (London, June 1984)

Not many nationalised industries are currently (or even very recently) loss-making. Those most suitable for discussion in answer to this question are the steel and coal industries. Whichever industry is chosen, some of the reasons for financial losses will be specific to that industry. However, the experience of a particular industry can aso be used to illustrate general points. Thus, for the British coal industry, we could say that losses have resulted in part from:

1. A lack of demand due to the fall in output in British manu-facturing industry leading to a slow-down in the growth in demand for power; the world recession causing a reduction in export opportunities and an increase in competition in domestic markets from foreign coal; the policy of the Central Electricity Generating Board to rely less on coal and to place greater stress than previously on oil and on nuclear fuel;

2. High costs of production because much of British coal output comes from old and deep pits which are expensive to work and which may not be suitable for modern automated processes;

3. An unwillingness on the part of mineworkers to accept the closure of large numbers of old pits, thus slowing down any move to large, new pits which would be cheaper to operate;

4. To the extent that the Coal Board has engaged in attempts to restructure the industry, considerable financial costs in redun-dancy payments and investment in new pits and processes.

We might then concentrate on arguments about costs and the restructuring of the industry and point out that whether or not present losses should be eliminated rests largely on an estimate of the social costs involved in closing old pits and in drastically reducing the workforce in the industry. Any estimate of these costs will rest on a number of assumptions. For instance, we need to assume something about how quickly (if at all) redundant miners will obtain other employment; what the effect of pit closures will be on the pit communities and the areas around the pits; what are the social and psychological costs of prolonged unemployment and so on.

We could use our *market optimists* and *market pessimists* positions from Chapter 1 to construct two extreme scenarios. One would argue that the displaced miners would soon find new jobs; that the increased competitiveness of the coal industry would contribute to economic growth; that people would easily and with little cost to themselves move from old pit areas to take up opportunities else-where. Market pessimists, on the other hand, would draw a picture of sustained unemployment of displaced miners, a high cost to the government in social security benefits, demoralised mining communities, lack of opportunity for young people, and a widening of the gap in income and wealth between the prosperous parts of the country and the old industrialised areas in the North, in Wales and in Scotland.

The answer as to whether the financial losses should be elimi-nated would depend on the estimate of the social costs involved and on value judgements regarding the importance of the distribution of income and of regional balance.

Chapter 4

1. Why and how may a government attempt to control the growth of private enterprise monopoly power? (ICMA, Nov. 1983)

We discuss at some length the arguments for and against monopolies in Chapter 4. There we point out two main arguments against. The first is based on the static case in which it can be shown that a profit-maximising monopoly will produce a lower output and sell at a higher price than a perfectly competitive industry with a consequent loss of social welfare (see Fig. 4.1 on page 62). The second is that monopolies, because they are not under competitive pressure, may not minimise costs of production. Thus, less total product will be produced with a given quantity of scarce resources. This idea is developed in section 4.4.3. We also point out that a movement away from perfect competition associated with increasing market power may give firms the opportunity of taking advantage of economies of scale, and the resources to undertake additional research possibly leading to more rapid technological change. The theoretical argument, then, does not produce a clear answer. We also hedge our bets regarding the evidence. In our summary on p. 68 we propose that although the evidence does not provide a convincing case for movements away from competition, movements towards greater competition are not necessarily desirable. For all that, there remains in market economies a presumption that monopoly power is undesirable possibly leading to the exploitation of consumers, a misallocation of resources and the development of managerial slack because of the lack of competitive pressure. A political point may also be made – that very large monopolies (especially if they are multi-national companies) may become more powerful than individual governments. *Private* monopoly power can therefore be seen as posing a threat to the democratic control of governments. Additionally, private monopoly power will have no incentive to take account of external costs and benefits and governments may have difficulty in persuading them to do so.

Governments may attempt to control the growth of monopoly power in a number of ways. They may seek to limit the growth of monopolies through control of mergers and take-overs (see pp. 69 to 71 for a consideration of British legislation in this area). Alternatively, they may seek to control the exercise of monopoly power through the limitation of restrictive practices which reduce competition or through public investigations of the pricing and output policies of firms with monopoly power. Yet again, they may pass more general legislation which aims to protect the customers of firms (such as the Consumer Protection Act of 1961) or the employees of firms. Governments may also attempt to influence the behaviour of firms with monopoly power through taxation and subsidy policies to try to ensure that the firms act in accordance with the public interest. Finally, of course, governments may convert private monopoly power into public monopoly power through nationalisation, though this does not overcome the principal theoretical objections to monopoly power set out above.

2. What criteria might be applied when assessing whether a merger between two firms was in the public interest? (London, June 1983)

Our starting point here is to consider how the enlarged firm resulting from a merger is likely to behave and the extent to which its behaviour will affect efficiency. Since 'efficiency' has more than one aspect in economics (see sect. 4.4.3), this suggests a number of criteria for assessing whether a merger will be in the public interest. Thus we can ask whether the merger will:

(a) interfere with consumer preference by seriously reducing consumer choice;
(b) lead to a reduction in output and/or an increase in price of the products of the merging firms;
(c) sufficiently reduce competition in one or more markets to allow the resulting firm to produce at a higher average cost, thus involving a poorer use of resources than before the merger.

One way of attempting to judge the reduction in competition involved is through product group or industry concentration ratios (see p. 43). An alternative is the more complex index used in American anti-trust legislation where the percentage market share of each firm in a market is squared and then the total is added up, thus putting much greater emphasis in the index on large firms. Such measures, however, only relate effectively to mergers producing horizontal integration. As we point out in section 4.2 vertical and lateral integration can also reduce competition. It is this which explains the very general basis of the definition of monopoly in British legislation. This concerns the percentage of the *supplying, processing* or *producing* of goods which a firm controls. We might also wish to enquire about the effect of a merger on the marketing outlets for rival firms; or we might wish to know the extent to which a merger allows the new firm to erect barriers against the entry of potential competition.

However, since there are arguments in favour of large firms (see for example our answer to this chapter's question 1), we shall wish to extend our criteria to include the effect of a merger on:

(d) the availability of economies of scale; and
(e) research, invention and innovation within the relevant markets.

But even this does not take us far. Any government in representing the public interest may have a number of aims which need not involve efficiency in resource allocation. For instance, it may seek full employment, regional balance and a balance of payments balance. It would then be legitimate to ask whether a merger would be likely to lead to:

(f) a reduction in the total level of employment in the companies participating;
(g) a rationalisation in search of lower costs which would increase regional imbalance in the economy;
(h) a stronger single company which would be more able to compete in foreign markets or to resist the challenge of foreign companies in domestic markets.

Overriding these may, of course, be the question as to whether:
(i) a merger may lead to the survival of a company which would otherwise go out of existence.

Other criteria along the lines of these last four could be proposed. It is easy to see why there is so much controversy surrounding the issue of whether or not mergers are in the public interest.

Chapter 5

3. Explain how a reduction in government expenditure, other things being equal, might affect the level of output. What difficulties are there in reducing government expenditure? (London, Jan. 1984)

To answer this question we need to know whether the economy is operating with greatly excess demand, full employment and rapid inflation. Assuming it is not, then traditionally one would expect a reduction in government spending, *ceteris paribus*, to reduce the level of output and employment. The reason for this is that a reduction in public spending is a reduction in aggregate demand for goods and services. However, the reduction in spending is also a reduction in someone's income, and since consumption depends upon income, it is likely that there will be further reductions in demand. The eventual reduction in aggregate demand and output is therefore likely to be greater than the initial reduction in government spending. This is known as the multiplier effect and can be seen in the following diagram where the vertical shift in the expenditure function represents the change in government spending, while the (larger) horizontal movement represents the change in income (i.e. output) (pp. 84–5).

In our diagram, the reduction in government spending (ΔG) leads to a fall in income from Y_1 to Y_2. From the lower quadrant

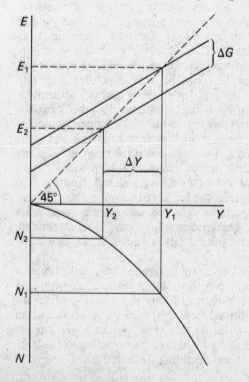

we can see that the level of employment required to produce this level of output has fallen to N_2 from its previous level of N_1.

Alternatively, if we knew the relevant figures involved we could calculate the effect as follows:

$$\Delta Y = \Delta G \times k$$

where 'k' is the multiplier. The size of 'k' will depend in an economy with a government and external sectors upon the marginal propensities to save (MPS), to tax (MPT), and to import (MPM) (pp. 84–9):

$$k = \frac{1}{1 - [MPC(1 - MPT)] + MPM}$$

There are three groups of difficulties encountered in the reduction of government spending. First, there are what might be called 'political' difficulties which arise because a large part of total public spending is on services which voters have said they wish to have provided by the state. In this provision they expect certain standards and have been quick to protest when public spending cuts affect education and health (pp. 94–5). Secondly, there are 'technical' difficulties, in that it takes time for decisions to reduce spending to be carried into effect. In many fields, e.g. defence, stopping and starting projects can be very expensive and very inefficient (pp. 93–4). Thirdly, there are 'economic' difficulties. Over one-third of public spending is estimated to be 'demand-determined', i.e. the government is bound by Parliament to undertake it if the demand is there. Social security payments and some health benefits are examples. This means that the range of spending which is eligible for cuts in the short run is reduced. More seriously, it means that if some cuts take place, and if output falls and unemployment rises, then the initial reduction in some government spending may be partially offset by increases in some other area of public spending. The tendency for (some) public spending to increase as demand and output fall is known as an 'automatic stabiliser'.

In recent years it has begun to be argued that reductions in government spending have very little effect on total demand and output (especially in the long run). This is because government spending 'crowds out' private sector spending. A reduction in government spending, would, on this view, permit lower interest rates and/or taxes, encouraging higher private spending to compensate for the lower government spending (section 7.5).

5. Why is the level of aggregate private investment unstable? (London, June 1983)

A profit-maximising firm will undertake all those capital projects which have a 'marginal efficiency of capital' greater than or just equal to the current rate of interest. In the diagram below, with interest rate r_1, all the projects up to and including I_1 will be worth while. Since, in the short run, capital equipment is subject to diminishing marginal productivity, a reduction in interest rates will be necessary to encourage firms to undertake more than their present level of investment. Thus we can say that, other things being equal, aggregate investment will vary inversely with interest rates and if interest rates fluctuate then so too will investment spending (p. 79).

However, when economists talk about the instability of investment spending, they usually have in mind its tendency to fluctuate for reasons other than changes in interest rate. This then becomes a question about the instability of the marginal efficiency of capital (MEC) curve in the diagram. To understand why the MEC curve is likely to shift from time to time, we need to remember its components (pp. 79–82).

The 'marginal efficiency of capital' means:
that rate of discount which has to be applied to the expected net earnings of one more unit of a capital asset, in order to make those expected earnings equal to the current supply price of the capital good.

The key words here are **expected net earnings** and **supply price**.

It is in the nature of capital projects that they earn a stream of income stretching away into the future. Because these earnings lie in the future it follows that they cannot be known with certainty.

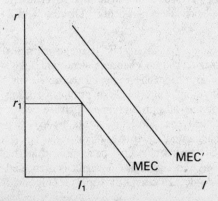

They can only be expected. If businessmen's expectations are subject to frequent revision, as Keynesian economists tend to think they are, then the MEC curve will move frequently: shifting outwards with optimism and towards the origin with pessimism. Some possible influences upon expectations of future earnings are listed on pp. 79–82. These include the outlook for demand in the economy, the outlook for the exchange rate and for world trade and the promises of governments – to curb inflation, promote growth, favour the private sector and so on.

The difference between earnings and net earnings lies in the deduction of running costs of the capital equipment. If running costs go up, all else remaining the same, net earnings will go down and the rate of discount which has to be applied (the MEC), etc., will be correspondingly reduced. Running costs may go up because of a rise in energy prices or in costs of imported materials and this brings in again the politics of the middle east and speculation about future exchange rates.

Lastly, although it may seem obvious that at the time of making the decision firms must know the supply price of the capital goods in question, it is possible for the effective supply price to vary as a result of changes in government policy on investment grants, and depreciation allowances. More generous provision will shift the MEC to the right and vice versa.

Chapter 6

1. 'Government borrowing is the enemy of employment in two ways. Firstly, government borrowing is inflationary which destroys confidence in the private sector. Secondly government expenditure "crowds out" private expenditure.' Discuss. (AEB Nov. 1983)

What the quotation appears to be saying is that government borrowing damages employment via two channels simultaneously. Note firstly that both lines of argument are opposed to the Keynesian idea that, given unemployment, high levels of public spending lead to higher aggregate demand and induce *more* private sector spending via the multiplier and the accelerator (pp. 84–6). We need to look at each line of argument in turn.

The first ('inflation') line of argument seems to assume that the borrowing is done in such a way that aggregate demand is increased beyond a level which the economy can currently supply. This *could* be true if government were to borrow from the banking sector by selling bonds or treasury bills to the banks. The result of this, other things being equal, would be to increase the money stock just as it would if anyone were to borrow from a bank (pp. 100–3). Then it would be possible to argue, in line with the quantity theory of money (sect. 7.2), that this increase in the money stock could lead to an increase in expenditure and that this increase in expenditure would lead to a rise in prices rather than output (sect. 7.4).

It is worth noting, however, that *in practice* governments have not financed their borrowing in this way but have sold bonds and national savings instruments to the non-bank public (pp. 107–8). This avoids the monetary expansion and the possibility of inflation but it opens up the second line of argument in the quotation, namely, that government borrowing 'crowds out' private expenditure.

The second ('crowding out') view is based upon three propositions. Firstly, that since the economy is always at or near 'full employment' in the market clearing sense, the public sector's use of resources has to be at the expense of the private sector (p. 188). Secondly, public expenditure financed by borrowing from the general public means higher interest rates than would otherwise be the case. Thirdly, these higher interest rates will make many investment projects unprofitable and so private sector investment will be lower than it would otherwise be (p. 108).

Once again, however, the evidence does not suggest that large government debt sales have been accompanied by high interest rates (p. 108). This seems mainly to have been due to the public's increased willingness to save, falling interest rates in other countries and the development of new, attractive types of debt by the authorities (pp. 109–10).

Lastly, it is worth noting that the two lines of argument we have presented are *alternatives*. Each depends on a *different* method of financing government borrowing. If either were ever true, it is most unlikely that both could be true simultaneously.

2. What determines public sector borrowing and what is its relation to the money supply? (ICMA, Nov. 1983)

The public sector borrowing requirement (PSBR) is the difference between the public sector's total expenditure and its revenue from taxes and charges in any fiscal year. It is the sum of the borrowing requirements of the central government (CGBR), the local authorities (LABR) and the public corporations (PCBR). The determinants of the PSBR are therefore the determinants of public expenditure and public revenue (pp. 98–9).

First among these influences might be said to be the public will. In democratic societies governments must recognise the preferences of the electorate for the proision of certain services by the state. If the preference is for a large public sector and if there is a reluctance on the part of the electorate to pay for these services by taxation, then the PSBR will be large.

The actual PSBR may still vary in size, however, even if governments plan to maintain it at a constant level. With constant tax rates and constant planned expenditure the actual PSBR will increase in a recession and diminish in a boom. This is because at constant tax rates the yield increases as more people are employed and pay tax and as more taxable goods are traded. At the same time, 'demand-determined' expenditure (on welfare payments and services, for example) falls. The reverse happens when economic activity falls (p. 99).

Lastly, it should be noted that governments in the past have deliberately varied the size of the PSBR, mainly by changing tax rates, so as to offset fluctuations in the economy. This counter-cyclical management of aggregate demand is based upon the Keynesian idea that any increase in autonomous expenditures works via the multiplier to produce a magnified change in aggregate demand, output and employment (pp. 82–9).

The connection between public sector borrowing and changes in the money supply rests upon the way in which the borrowing is financed. There are basically two options: borrowing from the 'non-bank private sector' (NBPS) and borrowing from the banking sector. The former has no effect upon the size of the money stock which is merely redistributed from the NBPS to the government in exchange for bonds and National Savings instruments. If, by contrast, banks lend to the public sector the money supply increases in the same way as it does if private individuals borrow from banks (pp. 101–2). In summary we can say that:

$$\Delta \pounds M_3 = \text{PSBR} - \text{(borrowing from NBPS and from abroad)} + \Delta \text{ bank lending to NBPS}$$

Recent research suggests that because of the way it has been financed public sector borrowing has not been a major source of monetary growth in recent years (pp. 106–8).

3. 'The quantity of money, the rate of interest and the public sector borrowing requirement.' Discuss the view that a govern-

ment can control any two of these but only at the expense of losing control over the third. (ICSA, 1982)

Public sector borrowing, interest rates and the supply of money are interrelated in such a way that if any two of them are determined (say, by government policy) the outcome of the third has to be accepted.

Let us assume that the government has a target for the rate of growth of the money stock. This rate of growth is determined by the rate at which the community increases its net indebtedness to the banking sector. The increase in indebtedness will be the sum of net borrowing by the private sector and net borrowing by the public sector (pp. 100–4). Let us assume now that the government has a given PSBR which it has to finance. The proportion of the PSBR which is financed by increased borrowing from the banking sector (and therefore adds to the money supply) depends upon how much of the PSBR can be financed by borrowing from the non-bank private sector. This may then depend upon interest rates. In summary, given a money supply target and a PSBR of given size, the government has to accept that rate of interest which will allow enough government debt (bonds and National Savings) to be sold to the general public to keep its own bank borrowing in line with the target for monetary growth.

To start the circle at another point, suppose the government wants to keep interest rates stable and also has to finance a given PSBR. Without raising interest rates it may find it difficult to sell debt to the non-bank public. Therefore it will have to borrow from the banking system and accept that in so doing it is adding to monetary growth. It determines interest rates and its borrowing needs but then has to accept the resulting monetary growth.

The final combination of targets arises when the government decides it wants a particular level of interest rates and a money supply target. If interest rates are fixed and government borrowing from the banking system is not to throw the monetary growth target off course, the total of public sector borrowing has to be kept to a compatible figure.

This last combination approximates to the objectives (and the dilemma) of the UK government in recent years. Being committed to achieving monetary growth targets and to keeping interest rates as low as possible to encourage investment, has meant trying to control (in practice reduce) the PSBR. This explains why these magnitudes feature so largely in the government's medium-term financial strategy (sect. 8.4).

How serious this problem is depends upon the interest-elasticity of demand for government debt (and ultimately upon the interest-elasticity of the demand for money). If the general public will buy more government debt only if interest rates rise significantly then there is a genuine problem for policy-makers. In recent years, however, the UK market has seemed willing to absorb large quantities of debt without large interest incentives (pp. 108–9). Lastly, it should be remembered that accepting a value for a third variable in order to achieve the other two, may be necessary for success but it can never guarantee it. Reducing the PSBR to achieve a particular rate of monetary growth and level of interest rates may be necessary. But if the private sector suddenly increases its own borrowing from the banking sector, the money supply target will still be missed.

Chapter 7

1. How might government capital spending affect private sector investment? (London, June 1984)

There are two views of the way in which public investment affects private investment.

The first, associated with Keynes, might be called 'crowding in'. On the assumption of spare productive capacity in the economy, an increase in government capital spending will increase aggregate demand, initially by an equal amount. This extra expenditure, being income to someone, will cause subsequent increases in expenditure. The ratio of the total increase in spending (ΔY) to the

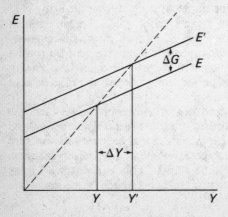

initial increase in spending (ΔG) is known as the multiplier (pp. 84–9). The process can be illustrated by the diagram above.

To produce the extra output, more capacity and therefore new investment will be required. This is the accelerator process. In addition, the extra government capital spending may raise confidence in many firms in related industries. The expected future yields from investment projects will rise, shifting the MEC schedule to the right. Again, more investment will occur at any given rate of interest (pp. 79–82).

The effect of the increase in public spending will be greatest if financed by methods which also expand the money supply. If it is not, then the government will have to borrow from the private sector which may mean interest rates rise, making some private sector projects less profitable (p. 130). Even so, on a Keynesian view, borrowing the funds from the private sector will cause only a slight rise in interest rates because of the high interest-elasticity of demand for money (pp. 116–7; 119). The public spending will still be expansionary.

The second, monetarist, view is sometimes referred to as 'crowding out' (sect. 7.5). Here, it is argued that whatever the level of registered unemployment, the labour market is either at or very close to a market clearing equilibrium. In effect, there is no unemployment. An increase in public spending on capital projects therefore must result in the use of resources that would have been used by the private sector.

In addition, it is sometimes argued that the method of finance is crucial. If the method of finance involves an increase in the money stock, there will be no displacement of private investment but, again, given that the economy is assumed to be at full employ-

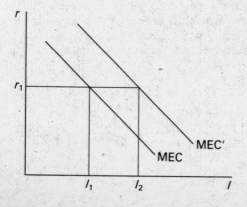

ment, there will be inflation. If, however, the government borrows from the general public, there will be a rise in interest rates. Because they argue that the demand for money is interest-inelastic, they expect the rise in interest rates to be so great that private sector investment falls to an extent which more or less offsets the increased government spending. In these circumstances, government capital spending has simply replaced private capital spending.

2. How is an increase in the money supply likely to affect the general level of prices and output? (ACA, June 1982)

Keynesian economists would argue that an increase in the supply of money relative to the demand for it, would cause people to buy financial assets since these are close substitutes for money. This would mean that the prices of such assets would rise and the effective yield would fall. New borrowing would have therefore to compete only with this lower yield (p. 118). In effect, current interest rates will have fallen. As a result of these lower interest rates, there will be some increase in demand for newly produced goods because some expenditures (typically on investment goods) are interest-sensitive. On the assumption of unemployed resources, this increase in aggregate demand will lead to higher output and employment. The three-stage process can be illustrated by the diagrams below.

On a monetarist view, the process begins similarly. In response to an increase in the money supply, people increase their expenditure. However, instead of limiting their increased expenditure to financial assets, people are expected to buy more of a wide range of assets, including consumer durables and capital goods (p. 114). Thus, unlike the Keynesian case, there is an immediate impact upon the demand for newly produced goods, regardless of the effect upon interest rates. The initial impact of an increase in the money supply is consequently much greater.

However, it is what happens in response to the increase in

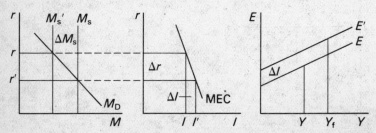

expenditure which differs more radically. Because the economy is assumed to be at or near to 'full employment' in the market clearing sense, the increase in expenditure cannot produce a rise in output and employment. It can only produce a rise in the general level of prices (pp. 121–5). This can best be illustrated by reference to the quantity theory of money:

$$M \times V = P \times T$$

If people spend the whole of any increase in the money supply on goods and services, this is saying that V above is fixed. Any proportionate increase in the money supply causes an equal proportionate increase in expenditure. If the state of the labour market means that the volume of transactions T cannot change, then the proportionate change in expenditure must produce the same proportionate change in the general level of prices.

5. What effects will a rise in interest rates have upon: (a) Business investment; and (b) The demand for money? (Oxford, June 1982)

There is little doubt that, other things being equal, a rise in interest rates will tend to reduce both the level of business investment and the demand for money but the size of the impact is a matter of some controversy.

Investment projects earn a return over a period of years. The initial cost is therefore greater than the immediate returns and therefore the funds have either to be borrowed or accumulated profits have to be used. In the former case, an explicit rate of interest has to be paid; in the latter the rate of interest is the opportunity cost of using saved profits for this purpose rather than lending them out.

Profit-maximising firms will undertake all those projects whose expected yield over their supply price – their 'marginal efficiency of capital' (MEC) – is less than the rate of interest. In the short run, additions to the capital stock are assumed to yield diminishing returns and therefore firms will only increase their capital stock beyond its present size if the rate of interest falls. Conversely, if interest rates rise, firms will reduce their capital stock by eliminating those projects whose MEC is less than the new rate of interest (p. 79).

The diagram below illustrates the effect of a rise in interest rates, but it also shows that the scale of the effect depends upon the slope of the MEC curve. That is, it depends upon the 'interest-elasticity'

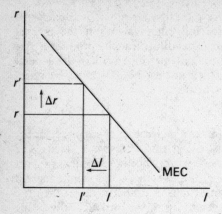

of investment demand. Keynesians traditionally take the view that elasticity is low (the effect is small) because many projects have a short-period pay-off and therefore the rate of interest is a small part of the total cost, and that 'confidence' in future demand for their goods is more important (p. 130). Monetarists, by contrast, believe the private sector to have stable and accurate views about the future and thus that interest rates are comparatively important in the investment decision.

On the demand for money, these views are reversed, though they both accept that since money (narrowly defined) does not yield interest, the rate of interest is the opportunity cost of holding money as opposed to other assets.

Keynesians regard the demand for money as interest-elastic. This is again a consequence of stressing uncertainty (pp. 117–18). Because people are uncertain they hold money balances for precautionary and speculative reasons. Thus part of their money holdings constitute a store of wealth and as a store of wealth money has many substitutes: government bonds, National Savings, stocks and shares. With such close substitutes, the demand for money will be influenced by quite small changes in the reward for holding those substitutes.

On a monetarist view, with less uncertainty, the money stock is held primarily for purposes of transactions for which it has no adequate substitute (p. 114). Given the lack of an acceptable substitute, people will need a very large interest rate inducement to persuade them to put up with the inconvenience of managing with smaller money balances.

Lastly, we can illustrate the consequence of combining an

interest-inelastic demand for money with an interest-elastic demand for investment goods (the monetarist view) and contrast it with the opposing (Keynesian) combination. Both pairs of diagrams below use a reduction in the money supply to cause the initial rise in interest rate. The diagrams show why monetarists regard changes in money supply as important while Keynesians regard them as less so.

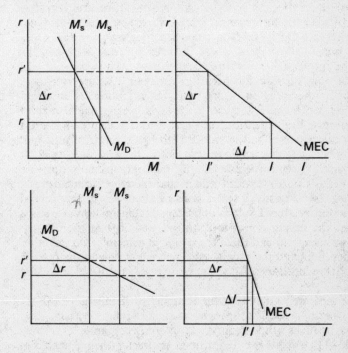

Chapter 8

2. 'Inflation is the single most important economic problem.' Discuss (London, June 1981)

The seriousness of inflation as an economic problem depends upon: (a) the rate; (b) the volatility of the rate; and (c) the degree to which inflation is 'anticipated' or 'unanticipated'. In the last ten years the UK has experienced rates of inflation varying from 24 to 4.8 per cent and for most of the period the rate has been below 10 per cent (p. 134). This is much less than the rates in some other countries (Israel, Latin America, and Germany in 1923–24) and may be well below the rate that is necessary to cause in practice the kinds of problem listed in many textbooks.

Inflation is often said to redistribute real income and wealth (pp. 141–43). This relies heavily upon the belief that inflation is unanticipated, i.e. that people cannot make contracts (to work, to supply goods, to save and to consume) which take the rate of inflation into account. There is little evidence to show that this happens in practice on a significant scale. There are very few groups of workers, for example, whose wages and salaries have not kept pace with inflation. Non-unionised, domestic workers are a case in point. All of those whose incomes are from state benefits have the protection of formal indexation. Many occupational pensions now provide for periodic 'revisions'. Where wealth is concerned, the greatest scope for redistribution is between borrowers and lenders because the loan is usually made in fixed money terms. But redistribution requires that the rate of interest paid by the borrower to the lender be below the rate of inflation. This has been the case at times, but not in the UK since 1982. It should also be remembered that the same groups of people are simultaneously borrowers and lenders and therefore simultaneously 'win' and 'lose'. Lastly, even if redistribution was in fact caused by inflation one would still need further argument to make this a problem. One might object to it on the grounds that the redistribution was arbitrary and therefore wrong in principle. On the other hand, depending on the way it went, one might defend the process because it 'reduced inequality' or, vice versa, because it 'increased incentives'.

Quite separately, it is sometimes argued that inflation confuses market signals, leads to people making wrong decisions and thereby reduces the general level of economic efficiency (pp. 143–44). Again, this relies upon transactors being unable to anticipate the current rate of inflation so as to make allowance for it in their selling and purchasing decisions. Given the level and quality of information publicly available, it is hard to believe that many people mistake nominal price revisions for relative price changes. Against this, it has to be said that mistakes are more likely to be made when the rate of inflation is constantly changing.

Under a regime of fixed exchange rates, inflation may be a problem for one country if its rate exceeds that of its trading partners (pp. 144–46). Its exports will become more expensive (imports cheaper). Given normal demand elasticities, the balance of payments will deteriorate and the lower demand will have adverse output and employment effects. In recent years, however, with a movement towards floating exchange rates, this is less of a problem, though, of course, if governments intervene to limit the degree of floating then some of the fixed exchange rate consequences could be reproduced.

It is also argued that inflation, anticipated or unanticipated, imposes 'costs' on the community because it diverts resources into changing price tickets, slot-machines and so on, and because it encourages people to manage with a stock of ready money balances below that which they would otherwise choose (p. 146). This is undoubtedly correct. The question is just how important it is. Estimates of the welfare costs involved, even by those who dislike inflation, are not very large, given the sorts of rates of inflation the UK has experienced.

Lastly, it has been argued, more by politicians than economists, that inflation causes unemployment (pp. 146–47). This is at odds with the traditional (Phillips curve) view and is at odds with the evidence since 1979 when inflation has fallen and unemployment has risen. Of course, one can make out a theoretically possible case through any of the mechanisms above. One has only to imagine, for example, that redistribution becomes so manifest and is judged to be so unfair that people give up working, or that people get so fed up with seeing the value of their money balances being eroded that they develop a system of barter with all the inefficiencies it involves. The fact is, however, that in practice, at rates of inflation like those experienced in the UK and in other Western economies, these things do not happen. Compared with the levels of unemployment which have been experienced and whose economic costs are relatively easily calculated, the 'problem' of inflation is probably trivial.

3. Explain the relationships which may exist between inflation and unemployment. (ACA, June 1983)

Traditionally, the relationship between inflation and unemployment was thought to be inverse. That is to say that at high levels of recorded unemployment prices would be stable (or even possibly falling as in the early 1930s); at low levels of unemployment inflationary pressures would build up and prices would begin to rise.

This view was associated with the names of J. M. Keynes and, later, A. W. H. Phillips (pp. 134–36). According to Phillips' examination of a long run of historical data on money wage increases and levels of unemployment, the level of unemployment at which prices would be stable, allowing for labour productivity

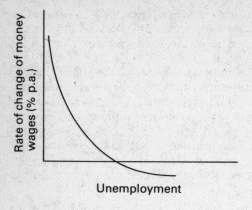

increases, was about 2 per cent. The diagram above summarises the findings.

The explanation for this relationship was that unemployment varied inversely with aggregate demand. As aggregate demand increased unemployment would fall until a position of 'full employment' was reached. After this point further increases in aggregate demand could not be met by further increases in output and so prices would rise until the existing output absorbed the whole of the increased money expenditure. The fact that inflation began when recorded unemployment was still positive (rather than zero) was explained by the existence of frictional and structural unemployment. It was accepted, in other words, that there was a level below which unemployment could not be reduced simply by increasing aggregate demand because there was inevitably some geographical and skill mismatch between the unemployed and vacancies and there would always be some people temporarily unemployed as they changed from one job to another.

The important point, however, was that the relationship between unemployment and inflation appeared to be inverse as a matter of historical record, there was an available explanation for these facts and this encouraged governments for years to believe that they could choose the 'best' combination of unemployment and inflation at which to run the economy.

In recent years this view has come under attack. The main assault has been via Friedman's 'natural rate of unemployment'. According to this argument, the labour market is always at, or is tending towards, a market clearing equilibrium (pp. 137–40). In the diagram, this is where the supply and demand curves intersect and the position of the curves will be determined by people's will-

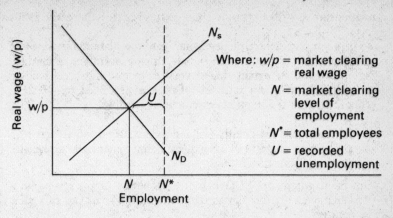

Where: w/p = market clearing real wage

N = market clearing level of employment

N^* = total employees

U = recorded unemployment

ingness to work (and therefore the incentives to do so) and by their productivity.

Two points are important. Firstly, those who are not in work may well be entitled to draw benefit. This depends entirely upon society's decisions about who should and who should not qualify for benefit. If the rules are fairly 'generous' and if the numbers recorded as unemployed are based upon numbers of benefit claimants, recorded unemployment could be quite high even though the labour market is clearing. This is shown by U in the diagram. Secondly, if the labour market is indeed clearing, then no amount of increasing aggregate demand can reduce the level of unemployment. Firms may try to produce more by hiring more workers and paying a higher money wage but with the price of all factor inputs rising, increased output will not be profitable. Equally, with prices rising generally workers will find their increased money wages amount to nothing in real terms.

According to this view, therefore, the level of unemployment is 'given'. There is nothing that changes in expenditure can do about it. Changes in money expenditure can only affect the general level of prices. Compared with the Phillips/Keynes argument we are now saying that unemployment and inflation are independent of each other, or that 'the Phillips curve is vertical' (pp. 139–40).

Lastly, it is sometimes said that there is a positive relationship between inflation and unemployment; that is, that 'inflation destroys jobs'. It is not clear what this argument is based on. Certainly, there is no factual evidence. In the 1970s inflation and unemployment were both generally higher than in the 1950s and 1960s but within those years the traditional Phillips/Keynes inverse relationship is still apparent. It is very clear for the early 1980s (pp. 136–7).

On a purely theoretical level one can speculate about rates of inflation which distort market signals, impair incentives, encourage barter to such an extent that normal economic life breaks down completely. But at no rates of inflation experienced by Western economies does this look even remotely plausible.

4. Evaluate the arguments for and against rigid adherence to a pre-announced rate of growth of a single monetary aggregate. (Oxford, June 1982)

The main arguments in favour of a monetary target rest upon a particular view of the causes of inflation. We shall call this view 'monetarist'.

According to this view, inflation is caused by excess demand and the level of demand in turn is determined by the level of people's money balances (pp. 114–5; 137–8). This is equivalent to saying that people hold money balances mainly for transactions purposes. If there is an increase in the money stock people will exchange money for a wide range of goods and services until the marginal utility of the last good acquired has fallen to the level of the last pound spent.

The effect of this increase in spending will be to raise prices rather than the level of output because it is argued that the economy is always at or is moving towards a full employment equilibrium. This 'full employment' is not to be confused with a near-zero level of recorded unemployment. Rather it is the level of unemployment (called the 'natural rate') which exists when the labour market clears (sect. 7.4.2). The level of output associated with full employment will not be constant but will grow slowly over time because of increases, for example, in productivity. Therefore, if we wish spending to keep pace with but not to exceed the supply of goods and services, then the rate of monetary growth should be matched to the long-term rate of growth of the economy.

The argument that the target rate of monetary growth should be pre-announced is that it improves the quality of information available to transactors and improves the efficiency of market behaviour (p. 149). Specifically it is relevant where governments are trying to bring the rate of monetary growth down to the rate of growth of output during a period of established inflation (p. 148). If people continue to strike bargains on the expectation of the established rate of inflation when monetary growth will not support such higher prices, people risk pricing their goods or their labour beyond what others can pay. In such circumstances there is likely to be unemployment until people match their behaviour to the rate of monetary growth. Publicising the rate should speed up this process.

There are three arguments against such a policy. Firstly, one may dispute the analysis of inflation. Galbraith (1975), for example, would argue that costs may be pushed up by trade union and corporate behaviour independently of the level of demand. Many Keynesian economists, though not going so far, would accept that some groups in society will endeavour to raise their share of national income before full employment is reached (pp. 136–7).

Secondly, one could argue that even if demand is the crucial factor, changes in expenditure may occur without corresponding changes in the money supply. People may use the existing money stock more intensively. Money balances lying 'idle' as a store of wealth may be lent out if interest rates rise, thus increasing velocity and the level of expenditure (pp. 115–9).

Thirdly, one could question governments' ability to control the money supply in practice. Because tight monetary control tends to be associated with high interest rates and these may conflict with other economic objectives, governments have often lacked the political will to carry through the policy. Granted the political will, however, there remain a number of technical difficulties. The system of monetary control in the UK relies upon influencing the demand for bank lending and this is not easy to predict. Government borrowing itself may lead to unforeseen changes in the money stock. Since 1976, UK governments have achieved their monetary targets with only a 50 per cent success rate (p. 148).

Guide to sources

The purpose of this list is to indicate sources that are readily available and which contain material at an accessible level of relevance to this book.

Government sources

The different branches of government publish a large number of statistical sources, the most important of which from the point of view of this book are:

Annual Abstract of Statistics (AAS) Central Statistical Office, PO Box 569, London SE1 9NH.

Bank of England Quarterly Bulletin (BEQB) Economics Division, Bank of England, London EC 2R 8AH. As well as providing detailed statistics on assets and liabilities of the institutions in the UK monetary sector, this contains in each issue a number of articles on economics, banking and finance.

British Business (BB) (published weekly) FREEPOST, London SWIP 4BR. This contains statistics and articles on British industry and on overseas trade.

Business Monitor (BM) Business Statistics Office, Cardiff Road, Newport, Gwent NPT 1XG. Annual, quarterly and monthly report series are published giving information on output, employment and costs of British industry by Minimum List Heading.

Economic Trends (ET) Central Statistical Office, PO Box 569, London SW1 9NH. Published monthly; often contains useful articles.

Employment Gazette (EG) Department of Employment, Caxton House, Tothill Street, London SW1H 9NF. This monthly publication contains both statistics and articles on the labour market.

Financial Statistics (FS) Central Statistical Office, PO Box 569, London SE1 9NH. Published monthly.

Monthly Digest of Statistics (MDS) Central Statistical Office, PO Box 569, London SE1 9NH.

UK National Accounts Central Statistical Office, PO Box 569, London SE1 9NH. Formerly (until 1984) entitled *National Income and Expenditure* but widely known as the *Blue Book*. Published annually.

As well as these and other statistical sources, government publications of use include:

Economic Progress Report (EPR) Publications Division, Central Office of Information, Hercules Road, London SE1 7DU. Published monthly by the Treasury, *EPR* often contains short but helpful articles on the UK economy or on the Treasury's view of government economic policy. Available free in large numbers on request.

Government Statistics. A Brief Guide to Sources. CSO Press and Information Service, Great George Street, London SW1P 3AQ. A free booklet listing the most important official statistical publications.

HMSO Government Publications, PO Box 569, London SE1 9NH. A monthly index of new government reports published by HMSO.

United Kingdom in Figures Central Statistical Office, Press and Information Service, Great George Street, London SW1P 3AQ. A pocket-sized abstract of statistics, free on request.

Banking sector publications

All the bank reviews are very helpful, publishing articles of current interest at an accessible level:

Barclays Review, Group Economics Department, 54 Lombard Street, London EC3P 3AH.

Lloyds Bank Review, The Editor, Lloyds Bank Review, 71 Lombard Street, London EC3P 3BS.

Midland Bank Review, The Manager, Public Relations Department, Midland Bank plc, PO Box 2, Griffin House, Silver Street Head, Sheffield S1 3GG.

National Westminster Bank Quarterly Review, The Editor, National Westminster Bank plc, 41 Lothbury, London EC2P 2BP.

The Three Banks Review, The Royal Bank of Scotland plc, Edinburgh EH2 ODG.

All of the bank reviews are published quarterly and they are usually available free on request.

Lloyds Bank also publish monthly:

Lloyds Bank Economic Bulletin (address as above). Each issue covers a topic of current interest. Available on request.

The Banking Information Service, 10 Lombard Street, London EC3V 9AT, produces occasional publications on banking and finance.

Other sources

British Economy Survey, Oxford University Press, Walton Street, Oxford OX2 6DP. Published twice yearly (October and April).

The Economic Review, Philip Allan Publishers Ltd, Market Place, Deddington, Oxford OX5 4SE. Five issues each academic year.

A more complete listing of available sources with a description of the contents of each source may be found in A Griffiths and S Wall (eds) (1984): *Applied Economics: an introductory course*.

Bibliography

Artis M J & Lewis M K 1981, *Monetary Control in the UK*. Phillip Allan.

Bain G S (ed) 1983, *Industrial Relations in Britain*. Oxford UP.

Beenstock M 1979, Taxation and incentives in the UK *Lloyds Bank Review*, Oct.

Beesley M & Littlechild S 1983, Privatisation: principles, problems and priorities *Lloyds Bank Review*, July.

Black J 1980, *The Economics of Modern Britain* (2nd edn). Martin Robertson.

Bootle R 1981, How important is it to defeat inflation? *Three Banks Review*, Dec.

Breit W & Hochman H M (eds) 1971, *Readings in Microeconomics* (2nd edn). Dryden Press.

Brittan S 1984, The politics and economics of privatisation *Political Quarterly*, Apr–June.

Brown C V 1983, *Taxation and the Incentive to Work* (2nd edn). Oxford UP.

Brown C V 1984, *Unemployment and Inflation*. Blackwell.

Brown C V & Jackson P M 1982, *Public Sector Economics* (2nd edn). Martin Robertson.

Coase R 1960, The problem of social costs *Journal of Law and Economics*, no. 3.

Cowling K *et al*. 1980, *Mergers and Economic Performance*. Cambridge UP.

Craven J 1984, *Economics*. Blackwell.

Creedy J (ed) 1981, *The Economics of Unemployment in Britain*. Butterworths.

Cross R 1982, *Economic Theory and Policy in the UK*. Martin Robertson.

Cullis J G & West P A 1979, *Economics of Health*. Martin Robertson.

193

Culyer A J 1980, *Economics of Social Policy* (2nd edn). Martin Robertson.

Dow S & Earl P 1982, *Money Matters*. Martin Robertson.

Dunnett A 1982, *Understanding the Economy*. Longman.

Elliott R F & Fallick J L 1981, *Pay in the Public Sector*. Macmillan.

Fiscal Studies 1985, A symposium on competition policy (February).

Friedman M 1969, *The Optimum Quantity of Money*. Aldine Press.

Friedman M & R 1980, *Free to Choose*. Secker and Warburg.

Galbraith J K 1975, *Economics and the Public Purpose* (2nd edn). Penguin.

Glynn D 1983, Is the level of government borrowing now too low? *Lloyds Bank Review*, Jan.

Goodhart C A E 1984, *Monetary Theory and Practice*. Macmillan.

Gowland D (ed) 1979, *Modern Economic Analysis – I*. Butterworths.

Grant R M, Shaw G K (eds) 1980, *Current Issues in Economic Policy*. Philip Allan.

Greenaway D, Shaw G K 1983, *Macroeconomics*. Martin Robertson.

Griffiths A & Wall S (eds) 1984, *Applied Economics: an introductory course*. Longman.

Hall M J B 1983, *Monetary Policy Since 1971*. Macmillan.

Hare P G & Kirby M W (eds) 1984, *An Introduction to British Economic Policy*. Wheatsheaf.

Hawkins C & Mackenzie G 1982, *The British Economy: what will our children think?* Macmillan.

Heald D 1983, *Public Expenditure*. Martin Robertson.

Heald D 1984, Privatisation: analysing its appeals and limitations *Fiscal Studies*, Feb.

Heald D & Steel D 1982, Privatising public enterprise: an analysis of the government's case *Political Quarterly*, July.

Highan D & Tomlinson J 1982, Why do governments worry about inflation? *National Westminster Bank Quarterly Review*, May.

Howells P G A & Bain K 1985, *An Introduction to Monetary Economics*. Longman.

Jackson D 1982, *Introduction to Economics: theory and data*. Macmillan.

Johnston R B 1984, *Demand for Non-interest-bearing Money in the UK*. HM Treasury.

Kay J & King M 1983, *The British Tax System* (3rd edn). Oxford UP.

Kay J & Silberston A 1984, The new industrial policy. Privatisation and competition *Midland Bank Review*, Spring.

Keynes J M 1941, *How to Pay for the War*. Macmillan.

Kuehn D A 1975, *Takeovers and the Theory of the Firm*. Macmillan.

Laidler D E W 1971, The influence of money on economic activity: a survey of some current problems, in *Monetary Theory and Policy in the 1970s* J C Gilbert, G Clayton & R Sedgewick (eds). Oxford UP.

Lipsey R G 1983, *An Introduction to Positive Economics* (6th edn). Weidenfeld and Nicolson.

Llewellyn D, Dennis G J E, Hall M J B & Nellis J G 1982, *The Framework of UK Monetary Policy*. Heinemann Educational Books.

Lloyds Bank Review 1980, Letters to the editor Jan. Apr.

Maunder P (ed) 1982, *Case Studies in Public Sector Economics*. Heinemann Educational Books.

Millward R *et al.* 1983, *Public Sector Economics*. Longman.

Morgan B 1978, *Monetarists and Keynesians – their contribution to monetary theory*. Macmillan.

Morris D 1985, *The Economic System in the UK* (3rd edn). Oxford UP.

Pappas J L, Brigham E J & Shipley B 1983, *Managerial Economics* (UK edn). Holt, Rinehart & Winston.

Peacock A 1984, Privatisation in perspective *Three Banks Review*, Dec.

Peacock A & Wiseman J 1967, *The Growth of Public Expenditure in the UK* (2nd edn). George Allen and Unwin.

Peston M 1982, *The British Economy: an elementary macroeconomic perspective*. Philip Allan.

Piachaud D 1978, Inflation and income distribution, in *The Political Economy of Inflation* F Hirsch & J H Goldthorpe. Martin Robertson.

Pierce D G & Tysome P J 1985, *Monetary Economics*. Butterworths.

Prais S J 1976, *The Evolution of Giant Firms in Britain*. Cambridge UP.

Prest A R & Coppock D J 1984, *The UK Economy: a manual of applied economics* (10th edn). Weidenfeld and Nicolson.

Price R W R 1979, Public expenditure: policy and control *National Institute Economic Review*, Nov.

Pryke R 1981, *The Nationalised Industries*. Martin Robertson.

Sandford C 1984, *Economics of Public Finance* (3rd edn). Pergamon Press.

Sandford C *et al.* 1981, *Costs and Benefits of VAT*. Heinemann Educational Books.

Savage D 1980, Some issues of monetary policy *National Institute Economic Review*, Feb.

Savage D 1982, Fiscal policy 1974/5–1980/1: description and measurement *National Institute Economic Review*, Nov.

Shackleton J R 1982, Economists and unemployment *National Westminster Bank Quarterly Review*, Feb.

Shackleton J R 1984, Privatisation: the case examined *National Westminster Bank Quarterly Review*, May.

Stanlake G F 1984, *Macroeconomics: an introduction* (3rd edn). Longman.

Stewart M 1972, *Keynes and After* (2nd edn). Penguin.

Trevithick J A 1980, *Inflation* (2nd edn). Penguin.

Vane H R & Thompson J L 1979, *Monetarism: theory, evidence, policy*. Martin Robertson.

Vane H R & Thompson J L 1985, *An Introduction to Macroeconomic Policy* (2nd edn). Wheatsheaf.

Index